Ordinary Life,
Festival Days

Ordinary Life, Festival Days

Aesthetics in the
Midwestern County Fair

Leslie Prosterman

Smithsonian Institution Press • Washington and London

To my parents, Albert M. Prosterman and Betryce G. Prosterman

Edited by Joanne S. Ainsworth.
Production editing by Rebecca Browning.
Designed by Linda McKnight.

Library of Congress Cataloging-in-Publication Data

Prosterman, Leslie Mina.
   Ordinary life, festival days: aesthetics in the midwestern county
fair / Leslie Prosterman.
       p.   cm.
   Includes bibliographical references (p.   ) and index.
   ISBN 1-56098-408-2
   1. Fairs—Middle West. 2. Agricultural exhibitions—Middle
West. 3. Folklore—Middle West. 4. Middle West—Social life and
customs. I. Title.
GT4607.A2P76   1994
394.6'0977—dc20   93-49385

British Library Cataloguing-in-Publication Data is available.

Manufactured in the United States of America

10 9 8 7 6 5 4 3 2 1
03 02 01 00 99 98 97 96 95 94

∞ The paper used in this publication meets the minimum
requirements of the American National Standard for Permanence
of Paper for Printed Library Materials Z39.48-1984.

The photographs appearing in this book, including the cover, are
by Leslie Prosterman, unless otherwise noted. For permission to
reproduce these photos, please correspond directly with the
photographer.

Cover image: Carroll County, Illinois (Figure 3.8).

Contents

Acknowledgments

The people I interviewed in Illinois and Wisconsin—the voices that speak in this book—are the reason behind this work. To preserve their privacy, I do not name the hundred or so people with whom I spoke, who gave me their time and expertise. In particular, the citizens of Carroll, Champaign, De Kalb, and Ford counties in Illinois and of Waukesha and Columbia counties in Wisconsin endured repeat visits and long sessions with me. I give special thanks to fair officials of the Sandwich Fair in De Kalb, who were most helpful; Phil Brady and his family housed me through a blizzard and arranged interviews during that time so I wouldn't miss any work. In addition, the people of Henderson, Livingston, and Winnebago counties in Illinois and Green, Green Lake, Jefferson, and Sauk counties in Wisconsin allowed me to observe and interview them for comparative purposes.

I am deeply grateful to the Department of Anthropology at the University of Illinois, Urbana-Champaign, for electing me a Visiting Scholar, opening the resources of the department and the state university to me, and providing colleagues who listened to me and stimulated my work: Edward Bruner, Clark Cunningham, Claire Farrer (now at Chico State), Paul

Garber, Thomas Riley, and the late Dimitri Shimkin. Larry Danielson (then in the English department at the University of Illinois, now at Western Kentucky University) and Kersten Danielson always supplied new ideas, willing ears, and nourishing ritual events. Judith McCulloh of the University of Illinois Press served on my dissertation committee and listened to readings of the manuscript; she and Leon McCulloh also extended personal friendship all through my research period. The University of Illinois graduate students in agriculutural economics, anthropology, and educational policy studies welcomed me for potlucks and mutual commiseration.

Around the region, my relatives always made me feel at home. June Weisberger-Blanchard in Madison, Wisconsin; Sadel, Herman, and Charles Levy in Chicago; and Doris Prosterman in Peoria and Annette Prosterman in Bloomington, Illinois, all expressed interest in my research, put me up when I was doing fieldwork nearby, and came for happy visits in Urbana.

During the periods of writing and rewriting, from dissertation to book, many people helped me in various ways. At the University of Pennsylvania (now at Indiana University), Henry Glassie heartened me from beginning to end. He always believed this work should be a book, and he made damn sure it would read like one—it's been a long process. John Szwed (now at Yale University) taught me that I should always be able to describe clearly and concisely what I thought I was doing. The rest of the faculty always encouraged new ideas and offbeat research. My entire graduate cohort demonstrated the actually obtainable ideal of supportive professional and personal relations. I was very happy to be at Penn in the late 1970s.

The two people who really hunkered down with the manuscript once I was serious about the book were Warren Belasco, University of Maryland, Baltimore County, and Gene Metcalf, Miami University. They read with a deeply critical eye; they did not stint on any comments and left me to make whatever mistakes I wanted. For crucial encouragement and advice along the way, I thank (in chronological order) Alan Jabbour, of the Library of Congress; Michael Owen Jones, of the University of California, Los Angeles; Pete Daniel, of the Smithsonian Institution; John Vlach, of George Washington University; Karal Ann Marling, of the University of Minnesota; Joanne Rappaport, of the University of Maryland, Baltimore County; and Hasia Diner and James Gilbert, of the University of Maryland, College Park. The following people read parts or the whole of the manuscript and made helpful comments: Kathy Neustadt, of Massachusetts; Brett Williams, of American University; Margaret Yocom, of George

Mason University; and Jane Young, of the University of New Mexico. Their collegiality was important to me. I particularly thank Margaret Yocom for the brainstorming session that led to the title of this book.

The Smithsonian Institution Press has been wonderful. From the first meeting with my acquisitions editor, Amy Pastan, through enthusiastic conversations with her and her colleagues Daniel Goodwin and Mark Hirsch and encounters with the proficiency and pleasant ways of the rest of the staff, especially Cheryl Anderson, Rebecca Browning, and Ann Dargis, I have counted myself very lucky. It has also been a joy to work with my copyeditor, Joanne Ainsworth, of New York City.

Carolyn Ferrigno, secretary of the American Studies department at the University of Maryland, Baltimore County, worked over the presentation of this manuscript many times in the last several years, always on last minute deadlines, absorbing new word processing and formatting requirements with aplomb. I owe her an enormous amount for her help and sense of fellowship. I also thank the rest of the American Studies department, Warren Belasco, Carole McCann, Pat McDermott, and Ed Orser for cheering on publication and for understanding when I was taking up Carolyn's time. We have all stood by each other so sympathetically through this, in part, because all five of us have published books in the last two years.

My close friends and family, some of whom I have already named, have also been wonderful. They supplied enthusiasm and patience, critical advice on writing and editing issues, and even source materials that proved helpful in developing the book. Nik B. Edes, of Washington, D.C., gave all of those things. Marilyn Goldberg, Kathy O'Dell, and Steve Braude, of the University of Maryland, Baltimore County; Lee Haring, of Brooklyn College; Cathy Mullen, of Concordia University; Judy Karasik, of Washington, D.C.; Barbara Charkey, of Keene State College, and Stanley Charkey, of Marlboro College; Brian Rusted, of the University of Calgary; Paula Johnson, of the Smithsonian Institution; my late brother, Steven Prosterman; my cousins, Michael Adams, of Albright College, Linda Miller, of Muhlenberg College, Jerry Levy, of Marlboro College, June Weisberger-Blanchard and Connie Blanchard, of the University of Wisconsin, Madison, and Bari Wood, of Connecticut, provided me with a web of assistance and fun. And my parents, Albert Prosterman and Betryce Prosterman, always urged me forward. One of my favorite moments in this whole process was when my father said, after reading the first manuscript, "Now I understand why you had to live there."

Introduction

The first agricultural event in my primarily urban life that I remember clearly took place somewhere in southeastern Pennsylvania. I was twelve, and among the activities at my Quaker summer camp were visits to various local events, one of which was an exhibition of local crafts, vegetables, and fruits in a Grange hall. Entering the building, I immediately felt tranquil. Part of this feeling came from the cool high-raftered wooden ceiling and white-painted boards of the Grange, a relief after the hot, dusty landscape outside and the swaying camp bus permeated with exhaust fumes. The boards of the exhibition hall smelled cool, clean, and old, and they did not move.

The intimacy of the exhibition and the sense of accomplishment embodied in the displays of jams and jellies and plant hangers and needlepoint gave me a feeling of satisfaction. The preserved tomatoes and other fruits and vegetables represented thought, planning, and care and collaboration with nonhuman natural forces—tangible examples of energy expended during the yearly agricultural cycle.

The small scale partly explained the intimacy. Clearly what was shown had been produced by local people who knew each other, judging from a wholly different kind of talk transpiring between them as we campers politely admired the surfaces of their work. The richness of this knowledge revealed itself in snatches of conversation. One needed a background of residence and time to understand who had carved a wooden bucket, whose skills had improved or declined since the year before, and the histories of aunts and grandfathers who had set the standard for excellence. People described how, at the last moment, the cookies in one rack completely burned and it was only by the grace of Theresa's six year old that the second batch hadn't gone the way of the first—and what was wrong with Theresa these days? They discussed Robert's struggles with the stock this year, Jim's last child moving away to go to law school, Rachel's triumph at the church bazaar, and other tantalizing morsels that seemed to indicate lives of integrity, integrity in the sense of wholeness: presence and coherence of necessary parts. The crafts, vegetables, baked goods, and animals that people made or raised; the arrangements of these items; and the people's conversations seemed to represent related concerns and thus fellowship and community.

Of course, this was a somewhat idealized vision—one I held instinctively and unconsciously as a twelve year old and consciously as an adult. As time has passed, however, I have come to believe that agricultural exhibition planners strive, consciously or unconsciously, for this vision.

In 1975, not too long after I finished college in upstate New York, during which time I had made annual visits to the New York State Fair, I was awarded an internship at the Folk Arts Program of the National Endowment for the Arts. Part of my job entailed reviewing past and current grant applications. I was struck by the number of applications to present what I began to call "constructed" folk festivals, festivals created by academics or administrators for the purpose of demonstrating or nurturing folk culture. These have an important place in cultural conservation, but at the same time I wondered why folklorists were not taking advantage of existing indigenous festivals like county fairs in order to showcase folk arts and folk culture. Even though folklorists pointed out some valid logistical problems of using such existing festivals, I looked for further answers.

Upon completing an academic literature search, I realized that very few people thought that indigenous festivals existed in the United States; as of the mid-1970s, scholars had found few folk festivals that they were willing to recognize, and of those, they had considered only a small number worth writing about. I was impressed by the attention paid to Latin American and European festivals as compared with the paucity of description and theory about the Philadelphia Mummers' and Louisiana Mardi Gras parades, holiday celebrations, family homecomings, and county fairs. I surmised that, in part, the lack of academic attention rendered the possibilities of using indigenous festivals invisible to presenters of cultural traditions.

Several years later I enrolled in the graduate program in Folklore and Folklife at the University of Pennsylvania. In deciding on a dissertation topic, I chose what I thought would be the manageable and interesting task of the cultural mapping and analysis of county fairs throughout the entire Mississippi River Valley (my academic interest in cultural geography not yet having extended to calculation of actual distances). I set out in the summer of 1979 to Wisconsin to survey the terrain.

Midwest America appeared to have the combination of the longest and strongest tradition of agricultural fairs in the country—it was America's heartland after all and, to some of us from the East, it was where "real" farming took place. I also felt a need to get out of the East, to learn about a new region of the United States. Some of the cultural assumptions there would, I knew, be foreign to me; even with relatives dotting the countryside in Wisconsin, Illinois, and Nebraska, I would deal with another set of values and beliefs.

American county fairs throughout the country display similar characteristics in their basic structure and aims.[1] Illinois county fairs epitomize the nature of the fair. Although county fairs exist throughout the United States, and have done so since the late eighteenth century, midwestern county fairs possess the most continuous solid record of operation in the whole country.[2] Wisconsin served as my first and comparative research site, but Illinois, as an agricultural state in the midst of the agricultural heartland, qualifies by right of its enthusiastic support of agricultural fairs to act as the featured state for this study.

Mass confusion characterized my impressions that first summer of fieldwork in Wisconsin. I felt initiated into the classic fieldwork mode; I could not find a lot of what was or was not happening because it was tacit knowledge. Still, even though I sometimes missed events and attended nonevents, I was overwhelmed with data. I learned that the midway was dead before noon. Late afternoon and evening proved to be the best fieldwork times of the carnival. Morning was the best time for viewing livestock judging. It took me some time to realize that I should be present when the dairy goats or market hogs were led out. Judging events often took place simultaneously. The choices I had to make between animals, categories of entries, and criteria swamped my notebook and psyche. And before I learned about criteria, I had to find out what everyone was doing at these events in the first place. At the beginning I never knew much about what was happening at any given time—the significance of the events nearly always eluded me; constant exhaustion from the unfamiliar welter of experiences sometimes sapped any desire to continue further; only doggedness, peach pie, and the premium book, which published the schedule of events, kept me going back to fairs throughout the lower part of the state.

Obviously, part of the problem lay in the confusion between perspectives. The only social cues I had to go on in the beginning were my own observations of the fair and "their" premium book. It took me a certain amount of time to figure out that there was a "mine" and a "theirs." Everyone looked much like me and we seemed to speak the same language. Even after examining the premium book, however, which printed the categories of the livestock, horticulture, food and crafts judging; the hours of the demolition derby, the Kiwanis barbecue, and the twins contest; and the prizes, or premiums, awarded to winning entries in each category along with a map of the fair, it took me a long time to match the information in it with life on the grounds. Life on the grounds included quite a few activities either not listed in the premium book or altered through word of mouth or posters; it was a folk structure. I needed ethnographic information to decode the structure of fairs, let alone their significance.

The next summer I went to study fairs in Illinois. I wanted to compare fairs between different states to see how much difference a slight change in region would make. As I drove down from Chicago, where I had been visiting relatives, to the University of Illinois at Urbana, where I was to be a Visiting Scholar in the Anthropology Department, the landscape provided more of a culture shock than anything had the previous summer.[3] The relatively treeless flatlands confused me and I got lost in the outskirts of a small town. When I finally sighted Urbana, it looked like an oasis. Trees shaded the streets and the frame houses. The streets curved faintly. I was so grateful for the familiar (to an easterner) topography that I instantly became quite attached to the town.

Over the next two years, the affiliation of the state university and the camaraderie of colleagues enhanced my field experience considerably. As an easterner, especially one who had grown up in Washington, D.C., I came under a certain amount of suspicion in the region. The alliance with a state institution helped in my acceptance by the people I interviewed and with whom I worked.

During that second summer of fieldwork the carnival workers, or "carnies," in the midway section of the county fair tempted me as sources for fieldwork. They were rough, exotic, and definitely "other." Sociologists and journalists had written extensively about the carnies' skittishness in interviews, their hidden culture. The prospect of getting the real inside story, especially as a woman, the prospect of earning my stripes through daring and brave fieldwork, attracted me.[4]

I steeled myself to interview the carnies, especially because the Smithsonian Institution had asked me to do so. They would feature American Talkers (auctioneers, carnival workers, and so on) in a section of the Folklife Festival in Washington, D.C., the following year. Through the next two summers I learned a great deal from the carnival workers, men and women. In time, however, it became clear that in a certain sense they were not the center of the action.

Although the midway flaunted the gaudiest sensory ticklers, the heart of the fair lay in the judging and exhibition. The most quietly intense energy seemed to rise from the rings, where exhibitors showed animals they had raised, and in the agricultural, art, and food halls, where they showed the products they had nurtured and created. The precision of the exhibition and the tension while exhibitors waited for the judgment of their peers compelled attention—if you knew what was happening and spent a lot of time at the fairs. I discovered that fairs exist because of local people's efforts within each county. The midway and the commercial section play essential parts within the total county fair, but the carnies and the product distributors do not fund, organize, or execute the fair. It is the Ford County or Carroll County farmers, insurance brokers, telephone installers, housewives, veterinarians, nursery school teachers, and craft store operators who meet year-round to plan the fair and make sure that it comes off. The place to find those people during most of the fair is the place where you find their work.

The judging and exhibition section of the fair houses the finished cakes, pies, jellies, string beans, 4-H projects, baskets, photographs, swine, rabbits, and poultry created by people from the county community and sometimes a little beyond the county in the case of livestock exhibitors.

This section also provides the locus for visiting, resting, courtship, posting of notices, and official and unofficial critical evaluations of people's work. Getting the chance to unwrap the meanings of the esoteric rituals and words reminded me of Alice in Wonderland: after many tries and what seemed like years after she glimpsed the little garden through the door, she finally figured out the right combination to get inside. Years after I first overheard the conversations at the Pennsylvania Grange, I started to learn the way in.

I worked in the field in the summers of 1979, 1980, and 1981 and from fall of 1980 to winter of 1982. With enough data for comparison between states and between fairs after the first two summers of fieldwork, I decided to focus on Illinois and Wisconsin county fairs. I relinquished the Mississippi River Valley.

I gathered data most actively during the periods July through mid-September (fair season in the upper Midwest) and November through March, after harvest and before planting. I attended twenty-four fairs in all in Illinois and Wisconsin. Following the summer of 1980 I narrowed the field to a sample of six specific fairs, four in Illinois and two in Wisconsin. I chose three fairs located closer to urban areas and three closer to rural communities; I chose two fairs in each of three topographical regions and in each of three slightly different climatic regions. With this sample I attempted to create a control for the more obvious factors of difference within the area, checking for idiosyncrasies. This study primarily draws on data from Carroll, Champaign, De Kalb, and Ford Counties in Illinois, with corroborating data from southern, eastern, and central Wisconsin.

Observation and notetaking, still photography, drawing, and interviewing helped me document the sensory features and internal patterns of the fair as a whole, as well as its component parts. Interviews at the fairs consisted of some talks with agricultural people on the fly, especially those in the audience at judging, those following judges around, or the ones sitting with friends of the exhibitors during visiting or leisure time. I recorded judges, auctioneers, and carnival talkers on the job. The mornings were good times to get more in-depth interviews of carnival workers and other transient fair participants, but most of the contacts I met at the fair were the agriculturalists whom I wanted to interview later in the year when they had more time.

From November through March of 1980–81 and 1981–82 (after harvest, before planting) I went from region to region, town to town, café to café, farm to farm, to conduct long, serious interviews. During the other months I interviewed some people and attended local events in the counties, such as the Shepherds Association Dinner, but the most intensive visiting took place in the winter. Other means of gathering information about my environment included photographing the landscape and listening to directions from people I interviewed about how to find my way in that landscape. The secretaries or presidents of the six designated fairs proved my best initial contacts. After I explained my job to them, they put me in touch with people who they thought were the most significant or would be the most helpful, and those people in turn connected me with others.

By the end of the fieldwork period I had spoken with more than a hundred people connected with agricultural fairs in east central and northern Illinois and southern Wisconsin. I talked to patrons (people who attend the fairs), exhibitors, judges, officials, and workers throughout the region. Often people would fill each of these roles in their lifetimes, either simultaneously (being a judge at one fair, a patron at another, a supervisor at yet another) or at different points in their lives. They could speak from more than one perspective. I spoke with children and adults, with feed salespersons, grandparents, soybean farmers, grade school teachers, sheep breeders, and a former minister of the church.

The interviews lasted anywhere from fifteen minutes to four hours. Usually they averaged two hours. In a few cases, I went back and interviewed people a second time, or I conducted an informal interview at a fair and a formal interview later in the year. Most formal interviews took place in people's homes, some in their offices or the county fair offices, some in the cafés where people met for coffee about 10 A.M. after they had completed morning chores. Most of the time I spoke with individuals or couples; occasionally a large group got together and shared experiences and information. I have changed the names of the participants to protect their privacy. All the people whom I interviewed affiliated themselves with the county fair. Therefore my findings apply to those people who declare themselves interested or involved in the fair, usually over a long period of time; the county fair appears to have little *direct* impact on others, although the fair does indirectly affect the rest of the county.

As far as I could establish in an anecdotal way, issues of gender did not seem to be dominant in understanding the functioning of the fair in people's lives or in how they participated in the culture of the fair. There was consciousness that gender roles were changing, but those role changes or role differences did not seem fundamentally to influence people's attitudes toward the fair or the symbolic dimensions of the fair.

Even though people clearly held different kinds of jobs and were at somewhat different income and education levels, their understanding of the fair's functions and the way they saw themselves seemed to be fairly consistent across these categories. Let me point out, however, that though the spread between income and education levels did not seem great, there did appear to be more owners or relatives of owners of farms and small businesses among the officials of the fairs.[5] The exhibitors, while not uniform, seemed largely middle class.

What more obviously did seem to affect participation were race and religion; with a few exceptions, the local and transient participants were all white Anglo-Saxon Protestants or Catholics. Family and neighbors constituted the essential factor; people stood a better chance of being involved if their immediate family or in-laws or someone down the road or in their church helped construct the fair. This involvement through family seemed true for carnies as well as locals.

The issue of insiders and outsiders seemed to be of interest to people in all parts of the fair. The county fair, with its carnival constantly accompanying its agricultural section, furnishes an arena in which people can play out issues of identity, of who belongs to whom and to what kind of way of life. I occupied categories of insider and outsider in relation to the agricultural section of the fair. I passed as an insider because I was white, American, middle class, affiliated with the state university, and had family from the region. I was an outsider because I was from the urban East with no ties to an agricultural way of life, because I was a single woman in her late twenties traipsing around the country, and because I and the people I interviewed did not at the beginnning share tastes and knowledge.

One fieldwork incident dramatized difference for me. Two women in De Kalb County kindly had agreed to give me information and preferred to be interviewed together. I arrived at a sunny kitchen in January and we sat at the table in the breakfast area just off the kitchen entrance. Coffee cups and coffeepot rested on the table, along with a big plate of cookies. One of the ladies poured out coffee for me and offered sugar and cream. The cookies sat there. I realized I did not know the rules of the society. I did not know whether I was supposed to comment on the cookies, reach for one on my own, or wait to be offered one. Were the ladies miffed that I had ignored their hospitality, a very important value in the culture? Did they think I had good manners for waiting? Did they think *they* had behaved inappropriately by including cookies in an outsider's working session? No one did or said anything about the cookies. The preoccupation in our voices on the tape is apparent as I valiantly conducted the interview with the cookies sitting in my consciousness as well as on the table. Finally, in desperation and with some knowledge of the importance of hospitality in midwestern culture, I broke into the interview and said, "My, those cookies look delicious! Are they for us?" The release of tension in our voices is palpable throughout the rest of the interview. That day my outsider status struck me with great force.

Because of this outsider status, cultural traits caught my attention and required my consideration. I learned to see landscape in the bigger sky of the prairies and to appreciate a new landscape on the ground. I also learned about the circulation of the ritual gift that was to be presented upon arriving at someone's house for a meal. I learned this in residence in Urbana as well as in interviews with people in other parts of Illinois and Wisconsin. Often one gift would circulate in different households; friends brought jams when arriving for dinner, which would then appear as a new gift when those hosts went to someone else's dinner. The criteria for acceptable gifts often were established tacitly at the county fair. This gift exchange helped me to understand certain components of the county fair and how both the exchange and the fair functioned to create social life in community interaction. In small towns in the Midwest, social life comes about as a result of paying a great deal of attention to active processes and participation, such as 4-H projects and picnics and breed association dinners.[6] The values that these midwesterners held in regard to living one's life became apparent.

The agenda for the interviews changed with the alterations in theoretical direction that developed during the period of the fieldwork. In the late seventies and early eighties the investigation of the county fair as festival seemed to be the obvious course for a folklorist. The loose theoretical notions that framed my fieldwork at the beginning in Wisconsin and then in Illinois led me to examine county fairs as intensifications and distillations of the values and activities of the local people. Festival theory appeared to be the most useful approach in determining the relationship between a yearly event and the year-round lives that built it. These theories indicated the possible connections between the carnival, the judging and exhibition, and the civic and commercial sections of the fair. But as useful as the concept of fair-as-festival was, it did not generate that resolved chord of a fundamental perception.

Right after I returned to Philadelphia from Wisconsin in 1979, I taught a folklore course at the University of Pennsylvania. At one point in the semester, I shared my initial experiences and observations about the county fair with the students. In the midst of a subsequent discussion about folklore and art, one bright student asked if the county fair as I had described it wasn't a lot like the art gallery I had been discussing with them earlier. After that question, I paid more attention in Illinois to the displays—both the static, like the rows of specimen phlox, and the kinetic, like the circling of dairy goats—of the county fair. I paid more attention to the ritual of the judging and the nature of the judgments. And when the fairs ended in Illinois in September, I decided to ask participants for a detailed account of every facet of the process of creation and judging of their work.

I began interviewing people in November, and the list of questions included inquiries about the item the person raised or created: where did they learn their skills? why and how did they bring their products into being in the particular way that they had? what criteria went into the making or raising of an item? was there a conscious discrepancy between the ideal and the execution? and what was the opinion of the judging process and the judges?

The fact that the fair and the system of judgments are expressions of folklore explains to some extent the significance of these phenomena in people's lives. I chose to study county fairs rather than state fairs because county fairs appeared to be constructed and used more closely by small communities of people. Folklore refers to those traditional expressive forms or arts, passed on unofficially and informally, and meaningful to relatively small groups of people. Folklore as a concept gains importance here because it highlights notions of art as communication, intention, and self-consciousness; the ability to construct form (mental or physical) rather than simply to receive it; and interpretation. It implies that people respond to their environment and control it to some degree, thus creating a dynamic interaction. This designates a process different from the elite, individually focused studio creation. Folklore highlights the person who shares or at least recognizes and admits to holding certain knowledge, understanding, beliefs, ideals, and values in common with other people. When county fair participants in Illinois enter, exhibit, and judge their work, they, in conjunction with the state government and various commercial associations, contribute to the development of standards for action in their world. The values, beliefs, and ideals of this group of people are revealed through a folk form they have helped to create. As a discipline, folklore begins its cultural exploration with the artistic text. In other words, folklore links up with literary theory and interpretation at the point of textual analysis. In this case, the county fairs and the thought systems expressed as aesthetic judgments form the text.

This point of uncovering culture makes the intersection with anthropology. Folklore and anthropology also share a methodology and politics, those of ethnography. Ethnography refers to the long-term direct observation of, participation in, and description of cultural forms. It includes the interviewing of people in order to understand a phenomenon from the perspective of the native as well as of the outsider. The importance of this last point surfaces in the political realm; respect for this perspective indicates a shifting of power and authority from the scholar-analyst alone to the intersection where the viewpoints of insider and outsider meet.[7] This whole issue of insider/outsider throughout the fair and in ethnography raises the question of whose voice carries weight. Who gets to articulate social values and ensure that they become the rule? Social values, ethics, and aesthetics (value and taste) are closely linked to each other and to questions of identity. Who are we to ourselves, who defines us, and how do we present ourselves to others?[8]

After reading a later version of this manuscript, various scholars commented on what an ideal world the county fair seemed, especially as I had portrayed it.[9] Where, for instance, they asked, were the farm closings that were such an issue during the late seventies and early eighties? I thought about that, along with the race problems and the other agonizing psychodynamics of communities. I had seen the down side of community life in Illinois and Wisconsin; how had I missed its role in the county fairs? Clearly my own fantasy of a harmonious and well-balanced world played an important part in my description and analysis of agricultural fairs. I concluded, however, that there must be a reason aside from my own desires why the county fairs emerged as such idyllic structures.

In some part the answer to this question lies in the desire of the creators of the fairs. I internalized some of the culture of the county fair that people create in order to postulate an ideal. Not only in interviews but in the whole structure of the county fair, the notion of harmony emerges and is insisted upon. Of course, the fact that this ideal is temporary and separate from everyday life indicates the participants' own acceptance of its difference from ordinary reality. But difference does not mean without impact. The construction of an ideal time and space, and the discussion of this construct in ideal terms without reference to conflict, reveals important values in this particular festival in these particular people's lives. The county fair represents a world they would like to exist and highlights rules of conduct, sets of judgments, from which they know they deviate but which reinforce a sense of togetherness in a fractured and strife-ridden world. Just as individuals deviate from the pronouncements of the judges but know and sometimes take comfort in the standards of the community, so the participants in the fair create standards for harmony even though they know that people are left out and that friends have lost their farms. It is not accidental that the nature of the aesthetic judgments echoes the nature of the world of the fair. The fair constitutes a statement of what life could be—a kind of cultural icon.

In this book I offer an examination of the symbolic aspects of a phenomenon of American culture in which many people have participated but which few have analyzed consciously or publicly. Scholars and popular writers have published a handful of articles and books on the subject; some fiction writers incorporate the fair into their pieces as settings or as vehicles for character development. But considering the pervasiveness of the experience of the fair in people's lives, it is odd that the comparative lack of literature persists. What I offer here is an illumination of some material, an aspect of the fair. My contribution emerges in the description of the fair in the seventies and early eighties, the focus on the facilitators of the fair, the analysis of a significant section of their activities (the judging and exhibition of agricultural and domestic products), the relation of this part of the fair to the others, and the connection between the aesthetic dimensions of the fair and points of everyday life for participants. Other people may have other perspectives—my own has shifted over time. As I write this introduction, I ask myself questions that were unknown to me during the fieldwork. I certainly expect readers to add their own ideas and questions to the reading. I expect readers to participate in the interpretation, using my data and interpretation as a point of departure.

The book moves between concrete and symbolic dimensions of the year. It begins with my description of the county fair in Illinois in the seventies and early eighties and includes its spatial and temporal aspects and the ways in which these aspects create a metaphorical as well as physical environment for fairgoers. Within these confines fairgoers sample a range of activities that reveal the essence of the fair. The history and contemporary structural organization of agricultural fairs come next, showing roots in the past and relationships in the present. Cognitive organization follows, with a narrowing focus on the categories in which exhibits are judged and displayed. Those categories are brought to life by the ritual of judging goods once they have been entered, discussed from the perspectives of both judge and exhibitor participating in cultural performance. From these cultural performances emerge criteria for evaluating things people make and raise. I then describe the ways in which participants use these criteria in their social and economic lives. Finally, I discuss how the conflation of festival and aesthetic criteria in everyday life leads to a vivid sense of place in a community.

This sense of place refers to both social and physical location for the local population. Interestingly, the barns and exhibition halls often seem dullest to the uninitiated outsider. In this section, the judging and exhibition of work entered by fairgoers to be judged by their peers goes forward. The action, if there is any, seems slow and often obscure. People sit and visit in the aisles and corners, and outsiders wonder if the judging is really open to the public. This judging and exhibition section is most meaningful and involving to the participant:

> The lumbering Holsteins are still the stars on Livestock Hill, where on 4-H Day little boys and girls dressed all in white pull balky heifers into the show ring. To fairgoers from Poughkeepsie or Manhattan, the children are cute, the heifers offer drama (will the half-ton cow bolt, with 80-pound owner attached?) and the judging quickly becomes as boring as dog shows are to cat lovers.
>
> To the parents watching, however, this is the fair's true moment, the crucible where some of their children become not merely willing helpers on the family farm, but aspiring dairy farmers.[10]

Rather than rely on surface glitz, local community members derive their pleasure from the intricate knowledge of people, techniques, and symbolic meaning. Here is an authentic, ordinary community festival.

Chapter One

The Aspect of the Fair

That blue ribbon has a lot to do with it.
They like that,
they like to compete,
and we have a lot of women who won't even put
*   their names on the tags,*
they don't care that anybody sees their name on
*   the product,*
but they just like to come and kinda compare theirs
*   with everybody else that's entered,*
and if they get a blue ribbon then
that's really exciting to them.

Paula Hornlein, Culinary Superintendent

Year after year the concentrated drama of showing and competition (a creative conflict of forces) engages the year-round energies of the people who organize the Illinois county fair(s) and those of their families, friends, and colleagues. The county fair provides a physical domain in which participants represent their lives to themselves and all other interested parties. They give shape to their values and skills with conscious imagination in a constructed time and space. Mrs. Denham, a one-time exhibitor and the mother, grandmother, and great-grandmother of current exhibitors, said, "There was a certain pride about it because we wanted to show off and that's what a fair is, a time to show and compete and sort of be proud of what you made and what your neighbors made."

From the perspective of local county participants, the fair as a whole exists to provide a focus to lives associated with agriculture. I found that focus sharpened in the judging and display of goods and animals that exhibitors brought to the fair to be evaluated. Those rituals of competition, known locally as judging and exhibition, dramatically enact participants'

Figure 1.1   Prizewinning canned goods, Champaign County, Illinois

cultural rules through and about art. The entire little world of the fair refocuses attention and reveals new ideas, combinations, and use for the larger world; the judging and exhibition does the same for objects, occupations, and creation. By locating in a time and space dedicated to a special purpose related to but removed from everyday life and by adopting stylized procedures, judging and exhibition reorder, highlight, and comment on the everyday occupational and domestic experiences of fairgoers' lives. The mundane commercial section and the burst of the midway play their role in this reordering and highlighting. This reordering, highlighting, and commenting fashions artistic experience for the fairgoer.[1] The county fair's temporal schedule and physical fairgrounds fashion a cultural map of when and where to find these heightened experiences for the initiated.

Time

County fairs in Illinois can last anywhere from three to nine days. Most often the fair begins on Wednesday and ends on Sunday. Currently, the fair season lasts from the first week in July, usually after the Fourth, to the end of the first week in September. The several days after Labor Day signal the end of the county fair circuit in this region. In former days, county fairs began in mid-August and went through October. Directors at a northern Illinois fair reminisced:

> It was an agricultural fair. You had this in-between time, before harvest, that the farmer could come to the fair.
>
> Most of the summer work was out of the way.
> The oats were gone, the corn wasn't ready to pick. . . .
>
> And the fall, to the farmers, was harvest time. It used to be, in horse and buggy days, the work never got done until way into the fall.[2]

Now, toward the end of the twentieth century, a variety of factors influence fair dates. The combination of possibly rainy and cold weather in the fall and the attempt to work around public school schedules makes summer "vacation" best for the fairs. Also, the current concentration on livestock judging at smaller fairs and the changes in the farming schedule, which puts the farming hiatus at the end of the summer instead of the beginning of the fall, have conspired to shift the fair circuit.

Community and carnival work together to set up the fair at the beginning of the fair week. This work often begins the night before the official opening. It continues through the next day in a stimulating welter of confusion. Those who find themselves on the fairgrounds at this point include themselves, perforce, behind the scenes.

Frenzied or quiet intensification of the normal pace adds to the excitement of the fair. Superintendents stay out long past their usual bedtimes making charts, preparing paperwork, directing the possible placement of tents and booths, and settling crises in preparation for the beginning of judging and exhibition. The morning of the opening of the fair reveals the carnies nailing their booths together and opening the trucks that carry the games. The carnies can afford to be more relaxed, since their active period comes later in the day. Commercial exhibitors fall between the poles of carnies and superintendents of competitive sections; they like to set up in good time to catch the crowds and greet passersby, but they do not feel the urgency of a particular slot of busy time.

The judging and exhibition rise to their peak of excitement and importance during the first three days of the fair, which usually occur early in the week. Most knowledgeable patrons turn their attention primarily to these events at this time. The judging is open to the general public, who often do not attend, either out of ignorance or a feeling of being left out. It is community members—exhibitors; friends, relatives, and neighbors of exhibitors; local residents, expecially those concerned with agricultural and domestic occupations; and fair officials—who attend. Casual visitors often prefer the midway, even though anyone can fill out forms in order to enter their goods in the county fair. Some committed exhibitors and many officials take time off to participate in the judging sessions, which include the organizing and judging of livestock, home arts, horticulture, agriculture, and arts and crafts. A few items that are worth less premium money, and thus are less important to the domestic economy, are judged on the weekend. Throughout the fair the buildings often surge with wandering spectators, but the atmosphere thickens with concentration most palpably in the first few days, during the periods of judging.

The beginning and middle of the typical five days of the fair tend to distinguish community-oriented events from spectator-oriented events. Locally produced concerts and variety shows draw their audience and players at this time. Fashion shows and 4-H or Home Extension demonstrations involve the same or a similar constituency as the judging does. Twins and freckle contests held in order to determine the degree of similarity and cuteness show the effort to make a formal presentation of the community to itself. These events are more publicly promoted, less arcane, and less specialized than the judging but still invite the active participation of the local community.[3]

By the end of the fair week, most of the judging has been finished. A few demonstrations and local events (especially horse shows) draw observers, but the weekend or the last two days of the fair really belong to the midway and the commercial travelers. This is when the biggest parades and spectacles take place and when the major country-western shows perform. Sunday might include a church service or special event, but it is officially the day when entrants take home their exhibits and pick up their premiums, or prize money.

At this point, local fairgoers spend less intensified time near the exhibits; now they go there to see which tomatoes took the blue or red ribbons, examine the peach preserves, inspect the Guernsey cows, visit with friends and reconnect with "their" space, and watch exhibitors feed their livestock. Exhibitors picnic with neighbors and relatives on the grassy sec-

Figure 1.2   Twins contest, Waukesha County, Wisconsin

tions near the Farm Bureau food stand. Sometimes the fair board schedules
a dance in the evening, but it is at the midway that most people congregate,
to play the games, eat so-called junk food, and watch spectacles with concentrated attention. The midway opens during the whole week, as do the
exhibition halls and the livestock barns. But the intensity of activity fo-
cusses at either one or the other pole at different times of the week or day.

The structure of the fair day recapitulates the week in many ways. The
early part of the day features the viewing and judging of entries into the fair
(such as dahlias, nut breads, Southdown sheep, and hobbies) starting at
eight in the morning. Most people present at this hour attend the judging.
The midway stays closed until noon. This arrangement not only makes a
clear space of time for the judging but gives the carnies a chance to rest
after their late nights. A few officials transact administrative fair business;
other patrons eat, visit in a desultory fashion, or simply wander around. Exhibitors break for lunch and then the judging continues until four or five in
the afternoon.

Between noon and five o'clock the community events begin, overlap-
ping some of the judging. The twins and freckle contests join barbecues,

charitable auctions to support the Muscular Dystrophy Association, and horse racing. Local community members (including exhibitors and officials) now consider horse racing to be old-timey, so they include it as a local event in their characterization of the fair. All these events are more public and more spectator-oriented than the judging, but they are enjoyed in a particular way by the local community. Community members often know or claim as kin the auctioneers or the other bidders in the Carcass Auction (an event in which entrants exhibit carcasses of animals they have raised in order to evaluate the "dressed" animal ready to be delivered to butchers; the fair then sells the carcasses at auction to restauranteurs or butchers—either to give the money to charity or to the exhibitors of each carcass); in the same way they are related to the exhibitors in the judging section. They gossip about the bids, or know who contributed the pigs for the barbecue or who is shredding the meat for the sandwiches. But they usually sit in a traditionally removed audience format or stand in line and have not shared the same experiences as the performers. That is to say, unlike the judging, they have not been auctioneers or participated in a twins contest. Participation is not the focus for the audience here. Partisanship is. The performers are doing something for someone else. This is a transitional period between local and cosmopolitan time.

Fairgoers relax, visit, and eat in the late afternoon. People from different sections of the fair investigate each other and the other sections. This is an intermediate period, when boundaries are crossed and public roles are temporarily left behind or made secondary.[4] This is slow time, a calm period during which carnies, commercial exhibitors, and agriculturalists sit and gossip, exchange news, and visit across categories.

In the evening, visitors throng the midway. They attend more distant spectacles like the demolition derbies, the country-western music shows, and the tractor pulls. Often, people come only for the evening, just as some only attend in the morning. Most visitors take in the whole fair, even while protesting that they never attend the midway or look at the commercial section. The carnies will have tested the site and figured out where the crowd will flow around their booths. This makes a cosmopolitan scene in the sense that diverse populations attend—fair patrons from the countryside, city, and nation. The midway provides an arena for licensed restlessness, loud ballyhooing, movement from one game to the next, and dislocating rides.[5] There is no particular time or place for stopping. The people halt only to focus their attention straight ahead on a spectacle or on a game, not to attend to their companions at their side.

Figure 1.3   Road to midway, Champaign County, Illinois

Time progresses on a continuum from more intimate, locally known and appreciated participatory activities to more public, cosmopolitan, passive events, such as watching a performer. In the middle of the day and the middle of the week, categories mingle and people circulate and pass barriers. Meals and idle viewing of the sights punctuate these periods. There are times for roaming. People and events move from private and intimate to public and more standardized forms of interaction. The level of activity maintains momentum at the ends, but the focus of action shifts from local to cosmopolitan, or from folk to popular culture. Time moves from binding, improving events to the licensed and anonymous events.[6] In the middle lies an interstitial time where the two forms meet and separate.

In the temporal structure of the fair, community and cosmopolitan concerns coexist, and sometimes they mingle. As in the physical structure, the activity in each time segment reveals clear understanding of the nature of those concerns. Fairgoers cross at the borders of the time periods. The structure of the week of the fair parallels the structure of the fair day. Periods of intense excitement alternate with periods of intense calm. The norm reveals a gentle rise and fall of activity throughout the day and week.

Figure 1.4   Fair advertisement,
Ford County, Illinois

Place

The excitement of the fair begins in the county seat with the appearance of eye-catching signs, banners, bumper stickers, and posters. These notices blare information with their boldface printing, bright colors, and arresting pictures of clowns, cars, singers, and outsize livestock. Merchants display in their stores cardboard advertising constructions for the fair, thus allying the town with the fair. These items list attractions and the times of the events. Local fair promoters paste bumper stickers to their cars with the name and dates of the fair. A few towns stretch banners across Main Street emblazoned with the fair's coordinates of name, place, dates. Some boards of directors of fairs have managed to obtain permission and sometimes cash from the state or county government in order to erect road signs directing passersby to the fair. These range from regular highway signs to

Figure 1.5   Entry banner, Carroll County, Illinois

unassuming homemade arrows at the turn-off for the fairgrounds. Step by step, closer to the place and date of the county fair, advertising grows denser. These indicators induce curiosity. They build anticipation. They mark off the range of the fair's allure.

Tall posts carrying a "Welcome" banner or little pillars serving as ticket booths signal the main entrance to the county fair. Arriving at the county fair gates, those guardians between ordinary life and festival life, I experience the imminent excitement of the fair. The list of prices and attractions posted at the entrance promises pleasures inside. Along with the judging schedule, which absorbs the attention of the knowledgeable and local fairgoers, the demolition derby, harness racing, the T. G. Sheppard Show (country-western music), and the tractor pull tempt those who seek spectacles on the other side of the fence.

Steel mesh, wooden slat, or chicken wire fencing circles nearly all fairs. At the least, a lane or road winds around the perimeter, connecting parking lots or empty fields. In this fashion, every fair constructs a middle ground that divides the known from the unknown, the probable from the possible.

From the entrance gates, several dirt, sand, gravel, or grass lanes fan out into the fair. One of these is generally wider and cleaner than the rest. It draws the crowd through the fair; it borders or becomes the midway and guides viewers through the stock barns and exhibition halls. These lanes resemble the yellow brick road in *The Wizard of Oz,* which suggests delightful adventures and significant understandings of the world.

Livestock are seldom to be found on this high road. Exhibitors keep them to the lesser lanes, possibly out of deference to pedestrians' sensibilities and for the animals' convenience. Authorities confine vehicular traffic to the margins of the fairgrounds in the interests of safety, tranquility, and cleanliness. The smaller lanes lead to out-of-the-way attractions, such as Civil War reconstructions and making-logs-out-of-rolled-newspaper machines. They act as arteries to the main road and normally get muddier and more rutted than the main road because of the heavier amount and heavier size of horses, cows, and trucks. Some of these arteries meander through the livestock area, in and out of the midway or past the food booths, halting in front of the exhibit buildings or ending in fields. They act as demarcation and as interstitial meeting places for the different sections of the fairgrounds. These arteries function as paths to attractions and as casual borders marking off different categories of the fair.[7]

County fairs in the Midwest are divided approximately into four categories: an indoor domestic, horticultural, and "small arts" section; a livestock portion with indoor and outdoor show rings; a commercial and civic section; and the midway/carnival.[8] The grandstand-track combination appears mutable, fitting itself into the other four categories when necessary. At times it houses some of the commercial or domestic exhibits, or it becomes the site of the 4-H livestock auction. Sometimes found scattered between these core sections of the fair are displays of machinery such as John Deere tractors or wood splitting machines, miscellaneous tents housing the Diabetic Club or the World Book Encyclopedia sales team, and a few food booths, like the doughnut stand with soft drinks, milk, coffee, and cigarettes for sale.

Canvas, wood, metal, cement block, and sometimes brick make up the built structures on the grounds. Some stand as reminders of the beginning of a fair perhaps ninety years ago. The white frame Home Arts building with cool green trim and the brick Stock Pavilion in a northern Illinois fair typify notions of permanence and continuity. The take-down crew demolishes the more ephemeral tents and wooden shacks and reconstructs them every year especially for the fair.

Figure 1.6   Home Arts building,
De Kalb County, Illinois

A narrowing focus reveals more details of the structures and their functions.[9] Builders usually make the newer buildings, especially for the showing of animals and domestic arts, of cement block, metal siding, or both. Fair board officials concede that these cheap, fireproof (and insurable) materials lack the picturesque qualities of the old frame buildings. They sadly cite expedience (money, especially) as the necessity for relinquishing the old-timey look.

The grandstand-track almost always (although not inevitably) abuts on the periphery of the fair. It helps form a boundary marker or corner because of its great height and breadth. Also, patrons of a specific grandstand event can reach it without losing themselves in the livestock barns.

The livestock barns lie at another edge of the fairgrounds, allowing for access of animal trailers and easier movement of the beasts. This location

Figure 1.7   Livestock barn with mural, Green County, Wisconsin

also partially isolates any attendant smells and dirt that might offend delicate sensibilities. The indoor exhibit halls tend to cluster, although occasionally one strays down the lane or toward the circumference. The fair office sits either on the periphery or in the exact center of the fairground.

Exhibitors house livestock in buildings consisting of a series of roofed
pens. The typical livestock barn is constructed of wood and contains several rows of stalls or pens made of horizontal slats of wood about four and
a half feet off the ground; two or three longitudinal aisles dividing these series of enclosures; and rafters, beams, and posts that support the corrugated
metal or wood roof. From the top of the stalls to the roof, the barns are
often open to the weather, and to fair patrons, inside and outside of the
building. The public can walk by outside and peer into the pens. The floors
are dirt and straw. In the center, or at one of the ends of these barns the
builders leave a large space. Usually intended to be circular, it is often as
wide as the whole barn. At its circumference it contains some benches or
bleachers. The dairy goats, sheep, and swine use this space as a show ring.
In some fairs, exhibitors show the beef and dairy cows here as well. If the
fair includes horses in its schedule, they live in barns that are entirely en-

closed on the outside. In rare cases, other, newer livestock pavilions are made of brick and also enclosed on the outside.

The fairgoer can find a show ring both under a roof and outdoors, if not in the livestock barns themselves. The freestanding indoor show ring is a building constructed from metal siding or brick, with few or no windows. These buildings rejoice in wide doors at the gable ends to permit the animals to enter and to leave with a minimum of irritating contact with each other and the buildings. The audience watches from bleachers set up on the periphery. Sometimes the superintendents erect brown or striped canvas tents, open at the sides for ventilation and exposure to the curious. Bleachers or chairs accommodate the viewers. Outdoors, a wooden rail, or a stake, or chicken wire fence, or in some cases, merely bleacher seats, mark off the show ring. Officials scatter sawdust over the earth in the middle for traction, to absorb excrement, and to keep down the dust. Some kind of seating arrangement (benches, bleachers, aluminum chairs) around the edge of the ring allows prolonged scrutiny of the action.

The grandstand and its track draws notice as one of the most visible features of the county fair. Usually the tallest and the broadest spaces, respectively, they carve out significant space from the fairgrounds. Only two out of eighteen fairs I observed lacked a track and grandstand combination suitable for racing and spectacles; these two provided spaces where patrons could view small events, but they were rickety affairs of wooden railings and nonraked benches.

The grandstand, often painted white with a gaily striped metal or canvas roof and multicolored pennants flying from guy wires, accommodates multitudes on its wooden or cement block seats. The space under the grandstand serves as an additional location for exhibits, food stands, and other miscellaneous booths.

Pride and necessity keep the green and brown oval of the track in front of the grandstand and in good condition. Good condition means smooth; free of roots, weeds, and stones; and earth of an even consistency, bordered by islands and lanes of green lawn to provide refreshment for the eyes. Green lawn is desirable and in short supply at the fairs. Visitors appreciate its cooling and peaceful effect, particularly close to eating and resting places.

The exhibit halls come closest to being "real" buildings. Each consists of four high walls, a roof, and doorways. They rarely include windows because every available vertical space needs to be used for exhibition pur-

Figure 1.8   Horticulture/Agriculture building, De Kalb County, Illinois

poses. Again, wood, metal, and cement block are the preferred materials of construction, painted white or light blue, sometimes with dark green trim. Most often the buildings are rectangular or square, but some of the fairs sport a hexagonal, octagonal, or round building.

Inside, banks of tiers or rows of tables display the accumulated squash and tomatoes, shocks of grain, dahlias, canned peaches and chocolate cakes, macrame plant hangers, 4-H exhibits on citizenship, and knitted baby coats. Officials utilize every inch of wall space. Superintendents consider the tension of so many more entries than space to be irritating yet satisfying. The irritation develops because officials and participants have definite ideas about how the entries should be seen and displayed. Such tight space constrains the implementation of these ideas. But so much response helps make a successful fair.

In both the livestock barns and in the exhibition halls exhibitors and officials of the fair create spaces for relaxation and social intercourse. As Ian Starsmore, a British industrial archaeologist, pointed out, "The fair is a technological village of extensive dimensions, but human proportions. . . . [E]ach fair is a way of life, as much a social gathering as a business enterprise."[10] People carve out little rooms or mark islands for a neighborly chat by arranging utility chairs in groups, stacking bales of hay, importing chairs and mattresses, or arranging personal effects to indicate the temporary use of space for socializing during the fair. Inhabitants invite each other to their spaces for drinks or to eat their meals or just to sit. They are known to be "at home" or in residence in certain spaces.

The commercial section of the county fair forms an interstitial category of the fair's arrangement. While the fair (in intention) primarily showcases the agricultural and domestic products of the local community members, the commercial section reminds the fairgoers of their place in economic and civic exchanges that they control less directly. This section consists of booths featuring political candidates (governor, state representative), sometimes political positions (anti-choice adherents), new developments in government (altered state driver's licensing requirements), educational organizations (the Apiary Society), and marketing opportunities and new products (home-sold cosmetics and variety distributors). I noticed that very few Democrats took booths at the fair; when I asked party representatives in county seats why not, they replied it would be a waste of time because the Republicans were firmly entrenched. Sometimes local residents sponsor and appear in one of these booths, but more often traveling or state representatives take responsibility for them. These booths partly demonstrate the negotiation of official and informal culture. Citizens must take note of official life, but they relegate this life to more marginal status during the fair. The fair emphasizes local community status.[11]

Exhibitors who staff these booths usually do not create or raise the contents or put them up for explicit competition to win prizes against other exhibitors as they do in the judging and exhibition section. These exhibits tend to be informational or initiate the first stages of a commercial competition or transaction; they might persuade customers to sign up to give a Tupperware party or order a supply of cosmetics. Any competition between companies touting similar products tends to be less explicit but more overtly commercial than in the judging and exhibition section.

Organizers of the fair give the commercial exhibitors a building similar to those housing the competitive judging. If there is a difference, it is in the materials of the building; when a choice must be made, the exhibits that will be judged will usually get the frame construction "old time" permanent building and the commercial exhibits will go in a metal siding structure. Sometimes, if sparse, the commercial exhibits will occupy a space inside the buildings that contain the competitive exhibits.

The commercial exhibits can also be found in tents or booths outdoors. If in tents, either a group or individual merchants will set up smaller tents for their own wares. Smaller tents and booths usually brandish striped or bright solid colors such as red or blue. Green-and-white striped or yellow-brown canvas characterize the larger tents. The fair nearly always rents these large tents from a local supplier.

The commercial section usually clusters in one definable section of the fair, with tendrils of commerce curling around and popping up in an isolated way in other areas of the grounds. The commercial or civic section reminds participants that mercantile and public life anchor the activities of the local citizenry but do not absorb their direct attention during the fair. The exhibitors of canned green beans, Hereford cattle, and macrame focus on the concerns and products particular to their immediate region while being kept aware of a wider world. In a sense, the commercial and civic section creates a conceptual and physical bridge between local and transient populations, between the judging-exhibition and the midway-carnival sections.

The food booths and tents follow the same metamorphosis from local to transient as does the commercial section. The booths range from the relatively stable wooden or cement block huts, some inside other buildings and some freestanding, to local efforts under tents or wooden stands with an awning, to trucks and edifices built of gleaming metal. These booths, paradoxically, are built of sturdy, permanent materials but are quite transient vehicles that will leave the fair. Their proprietors also sell the most evanescent food, such as cotton candy and fried crullers.

The fair food stands run by travelers on the fair circuit are never found near the livestock barns. The officials tacitly reserve these locations for the agricultural community; when vendors sell food in that area, they are local entrepreneurs or agricultural civic groups like the 4-H or Farm Bureau. Like the commercial exhibit halls, the local food booths provide a middle ground—a bridge between agriculture, local business, and the outside world. The transient carnival "grab joints," as the carnival workers call them, represent the outside world. The carnival core consists almost entirely of flashy fast-food stands.

The carnival structures vary, whether for food, games, or rides. Sometimes small wooden shacks open in front with a counter bisecting the space parallel to the ground. A carny hustles in the interior cavity. Usually the customer's efforts focus on the back of the booth or counter as he or she fires a rifle to hit a target or plays a short bingo game on the counter. These

Figure 1.9   Carny joint, Winnebago County, Illinois

stands (joints, in carnival workers' parlance) commonly front on an alley, arranged in rows. They resemble rowhouses.

Other booths or joints stand freely in the center of the midway. They form wooden parallelograms open from waist-height and with a counter running all the way around the square. Carnies operate games like tossing a ring into a goldfish bowl either on the counter or in the center. Many times these joints sport roofs or lengths of dirty but brightly colored striped canvas. Often, metal trucks transform into booths by opening a flap in their sides. Sometimes a wooden or metal frame and possibly chicken wire merely indicate or sketch a booth, as in the "Trial of Strength" or "The Dunker." Occasionally one finds a large trailer constructed as an interior booth dedicated to the purpose of displaying Elvis Presley's wax effigy, the haunted house, or the pygmies from Jamaica.

Carnival rides also constitute buildings on the fairgrounds. These huge eye-catching constructions of metal and plastic, these multimedia experiences mixing raucously poignant music, all-colored designs painted on the surface, and rapid turbulent movement, attract shifting and fascinated

Figure 1.10   Elvis in State, Green County, Wisconsin

crowds. Showmen pay great attention to the shapes and placement of these constructions. According to Ian Starsmore's observations:

> They [fairground machinery] have developed into unusual and sensational parodies of movements and forces, generated with essentially humorous and playful intentions by a vivid and adventurous attitude towards technology. . . . [M]any of the movements and objects experienced in everyday life have been exaggerated or expressed at some time in a fairground machine.[12]

The designers and operators take pride in how their Ferris wheels and bumper cars enhance the action of the riders and the riders' emotional perception of the experience. They also take pride in providing serious danger and lack of balance.

Each section of the fair is not abruptly defined. Sometimes, for instance, the commercial and food booths make incursions into the carnival or into crafts and domestic arts. Usually one element blends into another at the margins. Although an identifiable core proclaims the nature of each section, helping the fairgoers to organize their space and time, the edges

Figure 1.11   Carnival rides, Henderson County, Illinois

blur. The grandstand occasionally houses crafts and midway food at one end and leads to the stables at the other. Entrepreneurs locate machinery or seed displays around the edges of the animal barns, the car parks, the commercial buildings, and other "free" spaces. The 4-H hamburger stand might be next to the beef show ring, a rather explicit juxtaposition. One does not find, however, a stand of caramel corn situated in between the crocheted pillows and the baby sweaters. Only the interjacent areas permit this mingling to occur. The fair's structure retains the integrity of each core, conferring a distinct identity on each section of the fair.

Two parts of the fair that never mix, even at the margins, are the midway-carnival and the livestock section. The mingling of Chester White pigs and the whirling Cuddle-Up carnival ride is terrible to imagine. The unpredictability of pigs in particular and livestock in general, along with their aversion to sudden loud noises and inexplicable movements (the hallmarks of the disorientation of the carnival), render the carnival an inhospitable environment for the denizens of judging and exhibition. Room for experimentation rests on the boundaries, but the centers of the sections and the polar opposites of machine and animal remain inviolate.

Logistical reasons join conceptual reasons to divide the areas of the fair. Almost always, one outfit owns the carnival. It travels as a complete unit, taking on a few stringers along the way who will negotiate their carnival stay and operation directly with the manager of the carnival. The carnival sets up in an oval, horseshoe, or alley formation, according to the tradition and crowd sense of the manager, and according to the constraints of each fairground. The manager distributes all of the rides and games according to a prearranged plan. Incursions by outsiders into the center of this arrangement would violate a series of preexisting mental, social, and topographical concepts as well as commercial agreements.[13]

Other logistical problems relate to livestock. Animal traffic patterns require empty space between barns and near show rings. There must be no obstructions to free movement for urinating and prancing. Officials aim to minimize safety hazards to the animals or passersby. Complicated machinery (like Caterpillar combines) upon which small children can climb and from which they can fall indicates danger. The loud and raucous noise of midway activity disturbs the peace of the livestock that tend to shy at sudden noises and darting figures.

Not just environmental issues divide the sheep from the lamb chops. Everyone who goes to the fair or who participates in the organization of the fair identifies distinct entities that make up the total. Patrons indicate awareness of the interstices but describe the cores. Obviously the divisions that exist at the fair and in peoples' minds are significant. The sections reflect areas of interest and priority. People organize a potentially confusing event in some coherent fashion to reinforce patterns of ideal culture. Participants shape their concept of the world by the formation of recognizable entities; then they can apply this recognition in a new form to their own lives. This structure allows for the shading of boundaries, which gives an easier passage from one entity to the next, as Jane Turner, an exhibitor in Ford County, describes in talking about her husband's experiences with the commercial section and travelers, and her own concepts of categories:

All the extra stuff, commercial. It's sort of separate. In our fair it's in a separate building. It's in a merchandise building, well, the 4-H exhibits are in there and the grains and vegetables are in there, too.

I do go see the others, in fact, this last year, when Richard was helping with some of the dances, he would help close up that building, some of the

nights, and he got to know one of the exhibitors there, who was showing
leather goods there, and talked to him.

And he had been to different fairs and he was discussing the cost of the different items and what he paid for them and how he had to store it and haul
it and where he was going next. . . .

It's a mixture of local and nonlocal exhibitors. I don't know why I called it
extra.

Participants do not require air-tight boxes but rather general categories in
which they can manipulate their space and time. It is not a major conceptual upheaval to find elements of one category at the margins of another,
but to find an intruder in the middle would be disconcerting. The fair is or-
dered into islands and causeways. The first serve as loci for identification
and examination; the second serve as sources of discovery and travel. The
impression becomes one of apparently haphazard yet significant elements
encountered along a route.[14]

Exclusion and inclusion, outside and inside, emerge as one set of cultural meanings signified by this layout. One set of contrasts, emphasizing
shared values and ideals of local participants, opposes the midway to the
agricultural section of the fair. Local residents have complained about the
presence of rowdy, outlandish, immoral, or commercial elements from the
inception of agricultural fairs in America until today.[15] Because of the am-
bivalent reaction to the carnival, gathering verbal statements on carnival
going was difficult. Many dismissed the carnival because they deemed it
unimportant or claimed they did not go. In her research for her book *Blue
Ribbon,* however, Karal Ann Marling turned up an interesting discrepancy
between a Minnesota poll taken by the *Minneapolis Star* in 1947 and the financial records of the fair. The newspaper's poll asserted that only seven
percent of adults in attendance chose the midway of the Minnesota State
Fair as a point of interest, causing the pollsters to exult that most individuals were smart enough to stay away from "gyp" joints and overpriced freak
shows. The financial records of the fair, however, indicated that for every
dollar paid as entrance fee, another seventy-seven cents was spent on the
midway—displaying quite a bit more midway activity than most respon-
dents admitted.[16] My observation reinforced this statistic in the 1980s.
Local people whom I had seen earlier in the day exhibiting prize steers and

Figure 1.12   Map of the fair, Ozaukee
County, Wisconsin

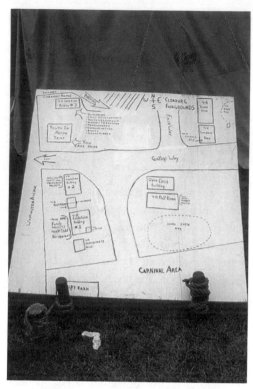

brownies were to be found later buying corn dogs and strolling around the carnival, even though they dismissed the midway in conversation.

So what role does the midway-carnival serve? Why do livestock breeders and mainstays of the household repudiate their interest in the carnival yet participate in its attractions? The well-known lure of the illicit invests the exhibition and judging section of the county fair, that distilled and expanded symbol of everyday life, with magic. The carnival attached to the county fair is a safe way to get thrills and to emphasize simultaneously the desirability of the ordinary. The reveler who patronizes the carnival in the context of the fair knows that his or her own world lies just a few safe feet away. But that world acquires an associational frisson by its juxtaposition to the uncertainty of the carnival.

This juxtaposition in itself creates titillation and tension, in turn raising adrenalin and focusing experience. The combination of the rural judging

Figure 1.13   Carny food truck, Winnebago County, Illinois

with the cosmopolitan carnival and related events like the demolition derby helps set the judging and exhibition apart from the everyday acts of live-stock raising, cultivating the land, cooking, and sewing that it intensifies.

The foreign qualities are significant. The foreignness or separateness of the carnival in the eyes of the locals is exemplified by a map drawn by one fair board in which a large blank space indicates the carnival as a foil to the detailed items of the rest of the fair. The simulated "streets" of the carnival refer to ordinary life, but life on the margins. Instead of the ideal of stable, supposedly reliable community rules of the small midwestern town, the carnies operate by trying to put one over on the "john" or the "mark," the outsider who is ordinarily the insider. The balls in the games are weighted, the wheels are rigged, the foreign patter of *ceeayzarnie* (carnie language) conceals the intentions of those temporarily in charge. The flimsy bright-colored tents and booths represent one-night stands; the trucks roll away quickly, leaving responsibility behind. These distinctions underscore the contrasts: the everyday values of the local community.

Even though farmers use machines, they see themselves as allied with nature. Thomas Jefferson extolled the ideal: "Those who labor in the earth are the chosen people of God, if ever he had a chosen people, whose breasts he has made his peculiar deposit for substantial and genuine virtue."[17] Agriculturalists celebrate nature and their connection to it at the fair. The conformation of sheep, the texture and shape of squash, the bunching of field grains, the taste of chocolate chip cookies, and the set of a cotton sleeve in a jacket are judged at the fair. Even when the jacket is polyester, the template is derived from the natural fiber original. Twins and freckles, judged in those contests, form natural phenomena. Even a beauty contest winner is judged on her "natural" good looks and deportment: "so unspoiled," "so charming," are the phrases often heard. The vehicular traffic is relegated to the margins in the agricultural section; animals and people reign in the center.

Apparently diverging from nature are the garishly beautiful machines of the carnival. The Chinese Pig Dog awaits visitors in his trailer. Neptune Subs features brightly colored sea motifs on the sides of the trucks. All of the carnival rides whirl and crash in a fashion surely meant to defy nature's supposed order while their decorations and music bring together colors, movements, and sounds seldom combined in the forest or on the farm. The road that leads through the carnival, the midway, allows the passage of cars and trucks but rarely animals. Wheel- or footprints rather than hoofmarks or manure mark the midway.

The surface contradictions between agricultural section and carnival include other opposing values that heavily weight one pole in each case. Permanent versus ephemeral, stable versus transient, directed order and effort versus aimlessness echo the categories and the judging criteria of the county fair. The value of stability over mobility for the members of the local community comes through in the difference between buildings. The Home Arts building often represents the signs of home, conceived of as permanent structures by the fair organizers with wooden shutters on the windows, exterior stairs with rails, and fixed wooden cases with glass tops inside. This picture contrasts sharply with the trucks and other booths on wheels and the rides of the carnival. The 4-H restaurant building might stand in the same spot year after year. Often a frame structure that represents a "real" building with white paint and a little lawn in front, the same organization runs the restaurant on similar principles from fair to fair.

This permanence and literal stability at one end of the fair seems to be emphasized by the fly-by-night qualities of the airy Tilt-a-Whirl, likely to be a different machine from last year. Certainly it will have been painted to look different and perhaps outfitted with a new sound system. And at the end of each fair the carnival machines get loaded onto a trailer to be hauled to some other carnival. The ride jockeys who operate the carnival rides shift locales most years, moving to different circuits or different machines. Indeed, during the winter, many of the male carnies are truckers.

Directed order versus aimlessness seems to be another separation between the judging and exhibition section of the fair and the carnival. During the mornings, when the agricultural section is hard at work either looking after animals or attending judging sessions, the carnies who work at night seem to locals to be shiftless and nondirected. They amble, they hang out on porch steps, they mug for girls and children. The local community members, who believe the morning is when serious souls get real work done ("Early to bed, early to rise, work like hell and fertilize," one livestock judge quoted to me), see the carnival as a place of sloth. And at night, when the carnies work hard, they work at games at a time when the "solid folk" play or go to sleep.

Another related seeming opposition is purpose and purposelessness. Members of the local community wander at the midway. They do not purposefully stride or head toward a particular destination. One livestock breeder said to me, "I always enjoyed the midway. We walk it now." Another said, "I like to walk down the midway and see people enjoying themselves." The physical setup of the midway, although apparently encouraging random stopping by, in fact quite deliberately directs traffic through its precincts. But in the eyes of those who create the fair and the patron from the other end of the fairgrounds, the carnival epitomizes the afterthought, the nonserious, the nonwork.

Physical shapes and arrangements further point up the difference between the hard, *directed* work of the agricultural concerns and the less-valued apparent randomness of the carnival. Straight lines will surface in the judging criteria for animals, quilts, and picture frames. The animal is often judged on the straightness of the back, the quilt on the straightness of the seams, and the picture frame should be symmetrical as well as straight. Grains and haystacks should be arranged symmetrically and stand upright. The carnival area resolves itself through circles and apparent lack of direction, as the agriculturalists see it. Machines on the midway literally shape themselves in circles and revolve—the Cuddle-Up, the Ferris wheel, and the merry-go-round. Roads wind around, presumably leading nowhere in particular, merely to another booth or ride.

Figure 1.14   Straight line of an animal's back, Bremer County, Iowa

The carnival "frames" the judging and exhibition; its qualities bring the judging and exhibition into focus. Picture frames give clues that something special can be found inside the framed space, and clues as to how to read the paintings found there; the carnival gives clues of apparent exaggerated opposition in how to read the judging and exhibition in the context of the whole fair.

Intimate control over the shape of the fairground, its buildings, and its temporal schedule forms artistic activity for those connected with the fair. "In diversity is unity; all phenomena are miniaturizations of the essential features of the universe".[18] The fairground creates a world apart that is a distillation of the everyday world. The streets; the little houses, barns, and huts; and the meal times and places for obtaining food reorder a larger world. In the judging and exhibition section we generally see sober, schematized recreations of farm buildings. In the midway we see the re-creation of the city streets: grids and circles. We also see the parodies of machines crashing into disorder, like the bumper cars or the Cuddle-Up, which throws the rider off balance.

Here the ambiguous and the fantastic hold a place, albeit a more obvious place, as they do in real life. The midway is the place for peculiar shapes, sounds, and behavior. The judging section identifies the location for the heightened experiencing of everyday activity. Ambiguous, mottled areas join clearly defined spaces, just as in the world. But at the fair, all these sections shine more clearly than in real life. The community world establishes itself in one area of the fair and the cosmopolitan world in another. Patrons can voyage actually and conceptually from one end of the fair to another. Space and time are arranged in a manner that emphasizes the varying worlds that intersect at the county fair. The layout allows for change, strangeness, and bewilderment, but the heart of the system is comfortingly apparent.

Time is another factor in creating a separate small world. Like the physical aspects of the fair's environment, the temporal aspect can be manipulated to form a reordering of "real time." Those who make the fair possess greater control over the structure of time in this framework than they do in many areas of their year-round life. The various officials can make up schedules and estimate proper allotments of periods in concert with participants. These blocks of time are arranged with a view toward accommodating the needs of different sections of the fair. Organizers embroider the texture of these times until they become densely concentrated spans of significant activity. In turn, this denseness liberates the participant or viewer from a dimly perceived routine into a new perception of that activity in daily life.

The special time and place of the fair make perceptible and concrete the assumptions with which participants lead their lives. They literally travel through a ceremonialized environment. This environment not only sets the stage for the ritual but surrounds the fairgoers with its ethos.

Whether it is showing animals, viewing exhibits, chatting with neighbors, or playing in the license of the midway, the particular activity sharply defines one or more planes of the living world. And it is clear that among other messages that the layout and schedule communicate, there is appropriate space and time for everything. The group planning and executing the fair grants itself, with historical sanction and administrative structures, the ability to marshal time and space in an orderly (or deliberately disorderly) fashion, outside of "real life" but intensifying it.

Chapter Two

The Past Made Present:
History and Administration

*The purpose [of the fairs] primarily (historically
and in the present) is to encourage and improve
agriculture in general within your county and
also home economics, for want of a better word
than that.*

*In other words, to encourage farm people and farm
wives to do a better job on their own individual
farms by coming to county fairs and seeing how
other people produce better livestock and can
better preserves.*

Joseph Sterling, official of the Illinois Association of Agricultural Fairs

History helps give depth to current efforts. Historical constructs can legiti-
mate action of the present. The weight of tradition and the number of people who have participated in related action in other periods give sanction to
the present. The choice of historical constructs and historical models legiti-
mates the organizers of the contemporary fair. The fairs did not spring out
of nowhere; they grew from European antecedents, which provided the
continuity and tradition from which to innovate. The mandate of the elevated or socially significant purpose has invested fairs from medieval times
to the present with a socially sanctioned reason for being—religion (Christmas fairs); commerce (horse fairs for buying and selling horses); work
(mop, or hiring fairs, held usually in the fall so that men and women seeking and offering employment could meet and come to terms); and education, improvement, and fellowship (agricultural exhibitions). In addition to
reinforcing everyday life or elevated principles, this type of mandate serves
to contain and thus allow entertainment to flourish concomitantly. Enter-

tainment draws patrons, but this "elevation" gives point to entertainment, just as carnival gives point to daily life.

In the past, the United States government mandated the agricultural fair as an institution that educated farmers in new techniques, developments, and methods. Education remains one major objective of the fair; farmers learn about agricultural, domestic, political, and technological innovations. Through its exhibits, the fair offers information to the patrons. According to Joseph Sterling, an official of the Illinois Association of Agricultural Fairs, the increase of suburban and urban patrons also has expanded entertainment (particularly harness racing), carnivals, grandstand acts, and musical attractions. These patrons can relate to such functions in a way that they could not relate to agricultural exhibitions.

European Fairs

A brief review of the historical development of fairs in Western civilization reveals a pattern that is significant in the understanding of American county fairs. Repeatedly, in different times and places, the confluence of trade, local ethos, diverse populations, entertainment, and religion or education has created the small world of a fair. Scholars agree that the word *fair* is derived from the Latin term *feria*, or holiday.[1] Thus, a fair is defined severally as a periodical gathering of buyers and sellers, in a place and at a time ordained by charter or statute or by ancient custom; in many cases fairs are resorted to for pleasure seeking by fairgoers as well as for business. Further definitions cite a fair as a festival or carnival where there is entertainment and things are sold, or as exhibitions, often competitive, of farm, household, and manufactured products, usually with various amusement facilities and educational displays. In all cases, writers admit that fairs are multimedia events, appealing to the senses and encompassing strange and familiar phenomena on a special occasion. They describe fairs as transient events with some permanent manifestations appearing year round.

Religious and economic factors were strong in the formation of fairs in Europe. T. F. G. Dexter believes that ceremonial games in prehistory and in ancient Greece and Rome became magnets for traders because of the holiday atmosphere and the numbers of patrons.[2] Other authors, like Cornelius Walford, agree, adding that the sacred feasts provided a time of truce or temporary neutrality in embattled times, enabling merchants to trade freely and safely.[3] William Addison cites Sir Henry Maine when describing small communities in pagan times living at perpetual war with each other. In their need for a neutral place to parley occasionally and proclaim inter-tribal laws, these small communities established regular "safe" boundary regions, which then served as centers for trade as well.[4] By late Roman times, it is known that wooden booths, stands, and tents were used at these religio-economic-legal gatherings. During this period and at this place of the suspension of everyday fears and hostilities, entertainers, purveyors of luxury goods, and the general populace displayed themselves and attended to special business.

Christian leaders and religious figures often are credited with the shrewdness to have remodeled Christian holidays and feast days to coincide with pagan celebrations. The scholars just cited on English fairs agree that the Norman church prelates early designated existing fairs as being under the patronage of the saint whose feast day fell nearest the fair day.[5] These authorities also split the honor of introducing fairs to England between the Romans and the Normans during their respective conquests. They credit the Romans with establishing fairs in England and the Normans with the linking of the fairs to Christianity. These English fairs were patterned after European fairs and served as one antecedent for the development of the American agricultural fairs.

From early British times until the eighteenth century, fairs served as a focus of trade. Monasteries often engaged in commercial activity by holding fairs in churchyards. Apparently the fairs were a detriment to religious observance, however, for both Edward I and Henry IV passed statutes forbidding fairs in churchyards or on Sundays and High Feast days except during the four Sundays occurring in harvest season. Still, fairs were recognized as furnishing a vital service to the country. Fair merchants were granted protection under the Magna Carta in 1215. By this time, many fairs had been legitimized and created through a royal charter. Given either to the church, the municipal corporation, or the lord of the manor of a district, the charter permitted a fair to be held in the district. Under its terms, the owner of the fair was held responsible for maintaining law and order at the fair, usually paying a stiff fee for the privilege. The charter laid down the dates of the fairs, provided protection against rival fairs, and gave the right to the owner to collect lucrative dues and tolls. The owner exacted these last for hiring stalls or ground space, for transacting business, and for transgression upon the rights of others. The merchants acquiesced in these fees and laws, since they then obtained a protected area in which to trade and exhibit. They also obtained the sanction of the fair as a seal of approval and belonging.

Fairs usually lasted anywhere from three days to several weeks. The fair was structured in the charters around the Eve, the Feast, and Morrow of a saint's celebration.[6] There were strict injunctions against prolonging a fair past the designated date. Many fairs apparently averaged about ten days in duration.

Religious seasons attracted fairs. Owners held mop, or hiring, fairs at Michaelmas in the autumn, the time for contracts to be made for the New Year. Provisioning for the winter occurred at these autumn fairs and at Christmas. The Christmas fairs entailed the celebration of the holidays and the last burst of entertainment before a long, bleak season. At Candlemas in February and at the Easter fairs, reprovisioning was a necessity. Fairgoers used these times to visit friends and indulge in high spirits depressed through the winter. Most fairs were held in the spring and autumn, although they were increasingly held in the summer as the nineteenth century progressed. These fairs stood as landmarks in the calendar.

Physically the fairs were held either in town streets or in fields. F. C. Roope, who was chairman of the Showman's Guild in England in 1964, feels that holding the fairs in public streets or fields emphasized the concept of the fairs as being open to all.[7] But alternatively it could be argued that these streets and fields recapitulated in miniature the world with which the fairgoers were familiar, in a smaller, more schematized format. Permanent or temporary structures were erected in the street, with a wide board in front for the display of wares and a room at the back for storage and living quarters. Owners rented these out at high prices. Those who could not afford a booth rented a space on the ground or wandered through the fair selling goods from a pack. If held in a field, the fair was laid out in "streets," where merchants could congregate according to their wares and where entertainment could be placed most advantageously to attract the crowds.

"Pie-powder" courts maintained order and administered justice at the fairs. The name derives from *pied-poudre*, the French for "dusty feet." These courts held summary jurisdiction over matters arising within the period and boundaries of the fair. The "dusty feet" refer to the speed with which traveling litigants received justice from their peers, who were usually participating in the fair.[8] They appeared in and left the courts with such celerity that the dust was still on their feet. These courts played a necessary role in maintaining order for the short duration of the fair and in mediating the quantity of disputes that arose.

The medieval fairs were "the common meeting ground of all classes, the places where men heard news of national events, compared grievances and caught the first breath of new ideas."[9] The fairs served a whole district and attracted constituents from miles around. The fairs functioned as a yearly outing, as well as an importer of scarce goods. Each fair became known for a specialty, such as cloth, horse trading, or hiring servants.

The purveyance of livestock, wholesale items, crafts, and durable goods, along with food and entertainment, eventually made up the heart of the English fairs. Cloth, wine, corn, sheep, fowl, butter, wax or tallow, rushes for bedding, in fact any surplus of eatables, raw materials, or crafts, were brought to the fairs, to be traded for money or kind. Men and women worked to have something to bring to the fair, in order to make a little money and participate. Locals traded side by side with foreign merchants and craftsmen. Vendors continually replenished pasties and ales in order to service the throng on fair day. Comfits made of sugar or containing gilt were in demand because of the festivity. Entertainment such as "Drinking, Music, Dancing, Stage Plays, Drolls, Lotteries, Gaming, Raffling, and what not" prospered along with strolling players and performing animals.[10]

F. C. Roope says there are three basic aspects of entertainment: human curiosity, the instinct of competition, and the desire for movement.[11] Peep shows, freaks, and fortune tellers pandered to curiosity. Games of skill and chance, as well as cockfighting and bearbaiting, aroused competitive spirits. The large crowds roaming through the fairground, primitive carrousels, and swings contributed movement.

As the sixteenth and seventeenth centuries progressed, more purveyors of amusements and entertainment benefited from the crowds in attendance. Booths featuring athletic feats, plays, performing beasts, dentists, giants, and other sideshows were established.[12] With the advent of the Industrial Revolution, communications and transportation began to improve, but it was many years before the full effect of this was felt by people and institutions. In the nineteenth century, local weekly markets carried more and fresher goods than previously. Traveling wholesale dealers also began to usurp some of the business that formerly had belonged to the great fairs.[13] Trade declined in English fairs, but entertainment assumed greater importance.

As entertainment came to predominate over economic, religious, or political reasons for the fairs or they lost momentum, however, authorities began to shut them down.

British Agricultural Exhibitions

In the mid-eighteenth century, the decline of the great fairs was paralleled by the rise of agricultural exhibitions in England. Agricultural change kept pace with major demographic shifts. Gentlemen farmers and large landlords were determined to eliminate ancient farming techniques and institute more modern productive methods. These agriculturalists formed societies to foster agricultural improvement (which included social improvement), and they produced agricultural exhibitions for the purpose of experimenting with and promoting new ideas for livestock, crop breeding, and gentility. Public exhibitions were one method by which agricultural improvers could disseminate their ideas. Premiums, to be won by competition, were offered as incentives to experiment and exhibit. Although these exhibitions were essentially educational and rural, they also stimulated social and recreational considerations of life from urban and commercial sectors as well as rural.

The Industrial Revolution furnished one great impetus for the new agricultural activity. Even though British agricultural historians now place the "Agricultural Revolution" as beginning as early as the mid-1500s in some regions and ending as late as the end of the 1800s in others,[14] most still agree that "the major increase in agricultural output must have coincided with the growth of population and the structural shift of the labor force from the country to the town in the course of the nineteenth century."[15] The movement of large new populations to the factories and cities meant there were fewer hands to produce food for a greater number of mouths. In addition, the frequency of wars and an increase in international trade meant that a new class, made up of soldiers and artisans and merchants, required food supplied from a shrinking rural population. Efficiency of production and a desire for profit became concerns of large landholders.

Old methods of farming, such as the three-field system (a communal system of farming, with strips of land or fields interspersed with neighbors' strips; also one field was often allowed to lie fallow, to rest the soil), common pasturage of livestock, and large numbers of uncultivated fields with little drainage or fertilization, seemed suitable only for producing small amounts for local consumption. Not until the mid-eighteenth century did large numbers of farmers work their own consolidated holdings of crops and livestock. This practice cleared the way for experimentation without fear that a neighbor's cow would mate with a farmer's blood bull, or that rows of beans and oats would become entangled with someone else's plantings.

Some of the great landowners could afford to experiment on a grand scale. They had the resources to put the results of their experiments into agricultural improvement; and they had an economic and social investment in feeding the new industrial workers. Agricultural improvement seems to have gone hand-in-hand with the development of an emphasis on the individual, artificial qualities (highly prized in the eighteenth century among the gentry) such as additive fertilizers and economic efficiency.

The major known "improvers" came from the ranks of the gentry. Jethro Tull developed a theory of cultivation, advocating drilling of seeds in straight rows instead of sowing them broadcast. He invented a drill to aid the process and published many of his farming theories and results in a book called *Horse-Hoeing Husbandry* in 1731. Charles Townshend, a former British secretary of state, began in 1730 to develop a four-course system of farming, alternating cereals, roots (especially turnips), and artificial grasses such as clover. The increased use of turnips through this system made it possible to winter larger numbers of livestock, supplying greater amounts of fertilizer to the land. Starting in 1750, Robert Bakewell experiemented with breeding livestock for meat rather than milk or wool. He established particular qualities in breeds that could convert feed into choice meats in a short period of time. Arthur Young, one of the foremost agricultural journalists of the late eighteenth century, commenced the publication of *Annals of Agriculture* in 1784, publicizing the "improvements" of the innovators. Thomas Coke of Holkham was an advocate and exemplar of intensive capital farming on a large scale in the late eighteenth century. He invested money and labor in the land, acquiring the latest machinery, draining fields, engaging in breeding experiments, and sponsoring farm demonstrations.

These agricultural improvers disseminated their findings through agricultural societies and exhibitions, of which they were the patrons. Those interested in farming attended these demonstrations to exchange ideas, inspect new methods, crops, and livestock, and to engage in practical demonstrations or competitions of plowing, wool spinning, or shearing sheep. Events such as the "Clippings" (sheep shearings) at Mr. Coke's estate of

Holkham and other farming festivals not only spread the word on the new manure techniques but invested the enterprise with a sense of fun and community. This was where the excitement in farming lay, proclaimed the festivities. Exhibits, demonstrations, learned papers, and a few competitions for prizes, followed by a dinner or ball were the order of the day.[16] To the degree that a handful of the elite could set an example, these events proved useful.[17]

In emulation of Coke, smaller landowners, tenants, and agents began agricultural societies, which were similar in purpose and operation to those of the Physiocrats in France at the turn of the eighteenth century. Neely quotes the *Gentleman's Magazine* of April 1799, which makes clear that the educated gentry were expected to be the participants. The categories for entry in order to win the gold medal include plans for ameliorating the condition of the laboring poor; building the most cottages on one's estate for laboring families, including a cow, hog, and "sufficient garden"; and satisfactory accounts, "verified by chemical experiments, of the nature of manures, and the principles of vegetation."[18] From the late eighteenth to the early nineteenth century was a period of intense interest in agriculture on both sides of the channel. Organizations formed in Europe at this time provided direct models for agriculturalists in America.

American Agricultural Fairs

After the American Revolution ended in 1784, farmers returned to neglected property. The alienation from Europe and England during the war and the lack of time to focus on agriculture contributed to the poor conditions that faced Americans in the late eighteenth century. The gap in information on new techniques in farming was remedied after the war by the exertions of major landholders of the period, such as George Washington, Thomas Jefferson, and John Randolph. Such men traveled to France and England to observe and then correspond with the innovators instituting changes in farming practices.[19] Jefferson wrote about a " 'System of Agricultural Societies,' the purpose of which is 'to promote . . . the diffusion of this skill, and thereby to procure, with the same labor now employed, greater means of subsistence and of happiness to our fellow citizens.' "[20]

Agricultural cohesion and improvement were imperative in America for the success of the new country. In Federal times the efforts of the major landholders brought the rather scattered and isolated farmers of colonial times into contact with each other. They formed societies similar to those in England and on the Continent. The first ones in America resembled academic societies, where members read learned papers. The average farmer had little interest in them and lacked the economic ability to compete. Agricultural improvement, as in England, required money and education for experimentation. More important, however, there existed few new markets for agricultural produce. Thus, farmers found little incentive to seek ways to increase their agricultural production.

The gradual democratization of those societies and the development of commerce in the United States encouraged working farmers to become actively involved in improving agricultural methods. Farmers who operated small holdings exhibited and viewed displays of livestock and produce in which theory had been transformed concretely into practice. Farmers could win premiums in competitions in areas that interested them. Sometimes as much as sixty dollars for the best bull and ten dollars for the best pair of fine woolen knit stockings were awarded in prize money.[21] Organizers gave prizes for sheep-shearing and plowing trials. Sheep shearings, similar to those events instituted by Thomas Coke, were especially important because of nationalistic and commercial implications. The raising of fine wool for cloth implied domestic self-sufficiency and the beginnings of a competitive trade base for agriculturalists. All of these early efforts petered out but functioned as forerunners to the present-day county fairs.

Elkanah Watson of Massachusetts was an early proponent of agricultural societies in America. As an owner of woolen mills in New England, he applauded the desire for independent American commerce and industry, particularly where it concerned woolen cloth. His interest in wool manufacture was shared by farmers and politicians, who patriotically wore homespun and imposed tariffs on imported wool. Merino wool was considered the finest, and when Merino sheep could be obtained, they became the focus of much interest at subsequent agricultural exhibitions. In 1810, after Watson's successful exhibition of two Merino sheep in the Berkshires, he engineered a large agricultural exhibition to promote major livestock development. Watson later wrote, "The other twenty-six farmers held back their animals in the vicinity for fear of being laughed at, which compelled me to lead the way with several prime animals." At the end of the day, after the exhibitors had arranged to meet again the following year, Watson apparently headed a procession that marched around the town square. Watson "stepped in front, gave three cheers in which they all united; and then they parted, well-pleased with the day and with each other."[22] As Neely says, "The interest had been supplied, popular support, though perhaps weak, had been exhibited, and certain distinct activities had been engaged in."[23] The following year's show included prizes for the best livestock and an annual address as well as another livestock parade, with participants wearing wheat cockades, sixty yoke of oxen drawing a plow held by two of the oldest men in the county, and a stagecoach filled with American manufactured products. Mechanics with their flag, marshals on horseback, and a band completed the procession. During the next several years, the organizers of the fair added prizes for agriculture, women's domestic manufactures, men's domestic manufactures, and diverse kinds of livestock. Watson instituted a pastoral prayer with the annual address and a grand ball to close the fair. This plan for agricultural improvement became known as the Berkshire plan, and the fairs became gatherings for entertainment and social intercourse, as well as for agricultural improvements and education. Fairs have followed a related pattern since, with rises and falls in the fortunes of agriculture affecting the fortunes of the fairs.[24]

The societies for which Watson established the prototype had spread into the South and the Midwest by the 1820s. Even though the agricultural societies attempted to serve the interests of all social levels of their constituents, however, it was still a small group of gentlemen farmers who organized and benefited most from the events. Few of the travelers' accounts or journals of this period name agricultural shows as rural amusements or as significant agricultural endeavors.[25] Most midwestern farmers with small holdings still lacked markets and were concerned with breaking ground and surviving the next several seasons rather than in improving production and quality of goods. Thus, agricultural organization declined to some extent between 1825 and 1840 as the country expanded. Public monies that had been allotted to aid the formation of the societies were withdrawn for lack of interest.

By 1840, renewed attention focused on agricultural improvement. The development of superior means of transportation and communication opened new areas for settlement and revealed new markets. As in England, sections of the country, particularly New England, increased their industrial capacity and their population. Growing numbers of workers needed food grown elsewhere. Because of war, famine, and industrialization, foreign markets opened to American agricultural products. Canals and railroads furnished means by which farmers could get their products to these widening markets. Inventors developed labor-saving machines like mowers, reapers, and threshers. Farmers perceived information regarding the latest agricultural matters as being necessary. County fairs provided that information.

The state and federal governments provided funds to aid the redevelopment of the now-extinct agricultural societies and to undertake agricultural research. These activities historically were founded and funded by private volunteers, but the increasingly complex social and economic organization of the country made these farmers solicit public monetary aid. At the same time, by mid-century, state boards of agriculture were evolving in conjunction with private local agricultural agencies. These reflected and supported the reawakening of interest in agricultural fairs. By 1860, there were many new agricultural societies.

Mid-century saw the regular gathering of groups with similar desires, welded into at least a temporary alliance for the furtherance of agricultural endeavor and social intercourse. Neely points out that in 1858 the commissioner of patents compiled a list of 912 state and county societies dedicated to the promotion of agricultural or horticultural interests, and in 1868 the Department of Agriculture listed 1,367 societies of this type. Neely goes on to say that in this period the Middle West had 443 of these societies, the southern states reporting had 165 together, New York had 97, and New England had 95; that is, probably half the active agricultural societies were in the Middle West:

> That these societies with their annual fairs were part and parcel of the expansion of the great agricultural Middle West is shown by the fact that the states of the Old Northwest—Ohio, Indiana, Illinois, Michigan and Wisconsin—with 22 percent of the population had 33.7 percent of the societies; and that the three frontier states of Iowa, Minnesota and Missouri with only 6.4 percent of the nation's population had 14.8 percent of its agricultural societies. The agricultural society movement spread from east to west, but pretty largely through the northern states.[26]

In 1868, following the Civil War, the Midwest still claimed the distinction of being the dominant flourishing agricultural region of the country. Here and in New England new agricultural societies and their fairs were created, even after the Civil War.

The scarcity of labor after the Civil War and the expanding industrial sector of the economy conferred more importance on agricultural fairs than they had enjoyed in the 1840s. At the fairs, farmers could find labor-saving devices and means by which they could improve quality and yield of their products to feed the increasing numbers of factory workers and city dwellers. There the farmers could acquire the new efficient agricultural machinery along with instruction on use and maintenance. In addition they could learn what kinds of purebred stock were being raised, what kinds of fertilizers yielded the best results, and what volume new seeds produced per acre. With the development of a larger population and a more complex agricultural-industrial economy occurred the need for institutionalized social organization. Warren Gates argues that the agricultural fairs of the turn of the century, "which reached a dispersed rural population whose isolation was ordinarily difficult to penetrate, provided a unique opportunity to apprise the farmers and their wives of current social concerns and efforts to accomplish change. . . . Socialization in consequence of a shared experience, annually renewed, offset rural isolation and contributed to a sense of community"[27] The agricultural fairs supplied information and examples illustrating new agricultural practices while they presented an arena for social gatherings and interaction. Thus, the establishment of social and economic codes of judgment and behavior was assured to those who lived on isolated farms:[28]

> The agricultural society was the paramount form of collective activity among the rural population and the fair the dominant institutionalized expression of that activity. . . . It was at the county fair that the farmer not only saw the means by which agricultural expansion was taking place and which he could use advantageously in bringing the land to a fuller productivity, but also gained a conception of his own importance and the inspiration for participating still more actively in agricultural expansion.[29]

The race track developed as a scene of social struggle during the 1860s and early 1870s. Debates raged in this period as to whether or not horse racing was to be a sanctioned portion of the fair. Some feared that the fair would be entirely given over to dissipated entertainment and politics.[30] The fair survived, however, with a balance of entertainment and agricultural improvement.

In the last three decades of the nineteenth century, agriculture and agricultural fairs underwent changes. Partly because of the increasingly intricate relations between agriculture and economic structures in a physically and industrially expanding country, late-nineteenth-century rural life called for a larger, more centralized agency like the federal government to organize certain facets of agronomy. More state boards were created, along with the United States Department of Agriculture in 1862. Many of the educational responsibilities became the province of the government instead of the agricultural societies and their fairs. Concomitant specialization occurred in the private sector, with division along economic, social, and political interests. Regional horticultural societies, dairymen's associations, wool growers, poultry associations, and breeders' organizations formed at this time. Politically, many agricultural societies split into Granges and Farmers' Alliances (forerunners of the Populist movement), and Farmers' Unions and clubs, and Farm Bureaus in order to deal with issues concerning big business, government, and economic and social life. By the beginning of the twentieth century, fairs, too, became more organized and encouraged more specialized compartments within them. Agricultural societies and county governments established permanent fairgrounds (often near towns or urban areas) and permanent structures and dates for the fairs. The societies allied themselves with business methods in making fairs, hiring managers to run them. The fairs became clearinghouses and outlets for some of those governmental concerns and specialized constituents.

With the growing use of the fair as a local central gathering place, entertainment played a larger part in the fair's avowed purpose, acting as a draw and a moneymaker; visitors and exhibits grew more numerous. Fair managers formed cooperative associations with other fairs to establish policies concerning carnivals, date setting, sharing of certain traveling exhibits, discussion of common problems, and standardized rules of conduct.

A crucial development of the twentieth century has come about because of the Smith-Lever Act of 1914 and the Smith-Hughes Act of 1917. The Smith-Lever Act brought the Agricultural Extension Service into existence. The extension service provides federal aid for agricultural and rural domestic education for adults in partnership with land-grant universities in all states and territories (known as Cooperative Extension Service) and with county governments (hiring county extension agents). In its own descriptions of its aims and programs, it stresses national leadership, policy, and programs implemented at the local level. The extension service has generated controversy. For many, it is an important lifeline to mainstream society, an educational and social course; it also creates a loyal constituency for many state universities. Others see it as a homogenizing, dictatorial force, wiping out local culture and autonomy.

Four-H is the junior division of the extension service. Encouraged by the Smith-Hughes Act, which grants federal assistance for rural vocational education, 4-H created a single national extension program in place of individual farmers' institute programs, which sponsored girls' and boys' agricultural clubs. Agricultural activities and results became relatively uniform in all the states, according to oral history, especially in the 1930s. By the 1960s, people were taking what they needed from the service and applying their own regional or familial spin on the information, as one sees later in county fair entries.[31]

The type of farming practiced at different periods has affected the look of the county fair. Through the late nineteenth century and until the latter half of the 1930s, farming in the Midwest was diversified. J. M. Dodd, a dairy science professor at the University of Illinois who was raised on a farm in southern Illinois, told me:

> They did their work with horses, they didn't have tractors so they couldn't do as big a volume of business.

> And they kept their own chickens and they had their own orchard and they had their own gardens and they milked a bunch of cows and sold cream to make butter and had pigs and raised their own colts to do the farm work.

Now, farms have become mechanized and more specialized. Farmers in the east central and northern regions of Illinois raise primarily feed corn and soybeans, or swine, or cattle. In central Illinois, the cash grain crop is so dominant that it is said to form the C, B, and F rotation, standing for corn, beans, and Florida. Recently, the rotation has also been called the C, B, and C, which stands for the Caribbean.

This change in farming effected corresponding changes in the county fairs. From the 1940s until the 1970s county fairs suffered a decline in participation. County fair participants cited the rise in specialization, laziness, lack of community spirit, television, and the automobile's dominance in society as the main reasons.[32] The specialization diminishes the number of potential exhibits because the soybean farmer buys milk and vegetables and meat at the grocery store, tills and harvests with machines, not horses and oxen, and buys household items at the shopping center. Laziness and lack of community spirit were often attributed to the popularity of television and the resultant ability to be entertained in one's own home and armchair. The automobile has had the opposite effect, conveying people farther away to urban centers, where they see more crowds, ingest a greater volume of information, and view more sophisticated entertainment than the county fairs can present. A final factor affecting county fairs has been the shrinking population of rural America. Now agribusinesses and fewer farmers run larger farms. There are, therefore, fewer rural participants to work in the fairs.

The 1970s saw a rise in participation. It used to be that agriculturalists would come to the fair and make a whole day of it. Now they come for shorter periods to fulfill many specific objectives. Sam Warren, a patron of the Sandwich Fair, said:

> We have a lot to offer the farmer . . . a general education that he can't get any other way.
>
> So we like to justify our existence from the fact that for what it costs the general public versus what general education costs the taxpayer, we're doing a pretty good job. . . .
>
> We're trying to offer an education.

Fairs are becoming increasingly oriented toward youth. This explains the rise of the junior show and entry categories. All fairs now contain two major classes under which all other items collect: open class and junior class. Adults (those over eighteen or twenty-one, depending on the county) enter open class. Junior class welcomes those under that age and over eight years old. Juniors may enter in any open show class, but no adult may enter in the junior class. A few fairs admit a senior citizen (over sixty-five) classification for which they waive the entry fee. Most fairs incorporate or rely on a 4-H, Future Farmers of America (FFA), or Future Homemakers of America (FHA) section. Only those participating in officially sanctioned 4-H or FFA/FHA programs may enter into those special sections.

Urban groups have become more involved in fairs since the 1960s. Periods of recession seem to help fairs; less money is available to spend on expensive vacations, and neighbors seem to care more about cementing community relations. Finally, the back-to-the-land movement and nostalgia, allied with economic constraints, have led people to grow more vegetables, can more produce, make their own clothes, raise their own animals, and present the results of those efforts at the fair.[33]

Organization of the Contemporary Fair

Participants cited education, financial incentive, and fellowship most often as reasons for entering and for spending so much time working to organize the fair. The great European fairs and the agricultural exhibitions supplied models for constructing current fairs to suit current preoccupations arising from the past. According to Gates, "Inclusion of commercial exhibits at agricultural fairs, a heritage of the European trade fair, was traditional and contributed meaningfully to the sources of ideas available to the rural community."[34] Participation in the fairs offers an education through doing and through seeing the results of doing on the spot. Older and younger exhibitors learn to prepare their entries, learn showing techniques, and learn business administration in the organization of the fair. The financial incentive can be defined as the promise of winning premiums and advertising one's expertise, but it also takes in the contacts and skills that those who administer the fair learn. At the same time, fellowship, especially in the form of family involvement and extended family/neighbor relations, intensifies in the organizational cooperation.

Local interested parties finance fairs in Illinois by issuing stocks or shares. This practice began in the nineteenth century, in some cases with a major reorganization occurring in the latter part of the century or in the twentieth century. Often members of the family pass down their original fair stock to their heirs. In Champaign County, out of a possible five hundred shares, the fair board knows the whereabouts of four hundred and seventy. At another successful fair, at Sandwich, Illinois, these shares are sought after; holders try to keep them in the family line. Frank Weaver, an official of the Sandwich Fair, said it is a matter of community pride:

> You can buy it [a share] from anyone who will sell it. They're extremely hard to get because they've been passed down . . . in the family . . . most of the time. It's extremely difficult to get any stock because nobody wants to sell it. Even though there is no monetary value to it a'tall, you see.

Shareholders retain the stock partly through sentiment and partly because these shares are one passport to eventual participation in the fair as directors. In every fair, a group of dedicated volunteers form the real basis of organization. This group (made up mostly of adults who usually are stockholders) constitutes a voting block that elects a board of directors, who then elect a small group of officers. The elections take place at a general meeting that stockholders and regular volunteer workers attend once a year. The fairs that have stockholders send out proxies for the elections held at the annual meetings and attended by local stockholders. If no stockholders exist, the assembled regular fair workers elect board members. Existing board members ask people they think would be good workers to run for a position on the board.

The board averages ten to fifteen members, and the officers of the fair usually consist of a treasurer, secretary, vice president, and president. The board members and officers of each fair most often earn a living as farmers, small-business people, sales persons for agricultural companies, or as otherwise self-employed workers who can manipulate their schedules according to the irregular demands of fair preparation. Those in other jobs, such as administrators for the utility companies, tend to take their annual vacation at fair season and work on fair business during their leisure time throughout the year.

Each county varies slightly with regard to how the fair and the board are organized, but the basic arrangement works on the principle that demonstrated commitment allows an interested person to participate at ever more responsible and exclusive levels. A scion of a "fair family" definitely has the inside track, but organizers welcome sincere, hard-working "outsiders." One board member of the Champaign County Fair said:

> If there's a vacancy on the board, we will usually pick someone who has demonstrated expertise in some field, but we're also looking for a person good not only in their department but capable of taking an overall view of the fair, the whole operation . . . Primarily all had an apprenticeship somewhere down on the ladder, helping someone.

In all cases the most regularly dedicated officials maintain control over the system but remain flexible in order to admit new talent. They are realistic about the situation. Families inherit many of the positions on the boards or in management. This does not mean that children automatically take the position with no apprenticeship or work, but if children show interest and make an effort, then they virtually assure themselves of a position. One man told me:

> I'd hate to say that nepotism rules . . . however, from a practical standpoint, because the individual's family often is interested in the fair, they have to

be, they then gradually grow up in it, so if they're in a position to assume it, yes, there's no question, you do have a lot of relationship.

Some boards are more active than others. In one fair, each board member officiates as the superintendent of at least one part of the fair. In another, only the president and nonboard-member superintendents contribute significantly. Some boards meet regularly four times a year, apart from other business, while other boards meet perfunctorily once a year. Still, those actually responsible for producing the fair meet, talk, and remain active constantly throughout the year. A former board member of the Ford County Fair, Philip Clarke said, "We see a need for a meeting, we just start getting together on the phone or paper or whatever and send cards out and call a meeting."

The board members oversee financial angles of the fair and building projects, along with year-round maintenance of the physical plant, relations with other fairs, and relations with federal and state agencies. They obtain entertainment, such as country-western singing groups for the grandstand and carnivals and clowns for the midway, and negotiate with traveling and local commercial groups. They take care of public relations, and they initiate new attractions, like midget tractor pulls.

The board handles the finances of the county fair. Insurance ranks as one of the greatest expenditures of the fair. This constitutes a perpetual headache for fair boards. "If anything's going to break the fairs, it'll be insurance. We pay $4,300 a year liability alone, can't do without it. Also need building insurance," bemoaned Philip Clarke. Utilities costs rise every year and make it difficult to plan a budget. Although most of the fair's workers volunteer, the fair board employs some paid help for maintenance, security, and special secretarial duties. The fair board meets these costs during the year. The fair incurs a large percentage of the expenditures, however, during the one week of fair season. During fair week, the fair board pays out premiums, employs special help for the fair, pays judges' fees, pays for the sound system and tent rentals, and pays for the performers in the grandstand. All those expenditures require cash up front; the money must be disbursed before the end of the fair.

The fair derives its income from many sources. Off-season rental of the fairgrounds and buildings increasingly provides a means of funding the physical plant and general upkeep of year-round fair administration. But the largest single source of income comes from fees at the entry gate. Gen-

Figure 2.1   Ticket booth, Winnebago County, Illinois

eral admission supplies more than half of the revenue of most county fairs. The rental of space to carnival and concession operators, plus a percentage of their gate fees, supply a sizable percentage of money. The rental of indoor and outdoor space for exhibits and of utilities brings in more. In addition, the exhibitors of all materials must pay at least a small entry fee, in some cases as little as fifty cents.

Charges for special grandstand events like demolition derbies and country-western music shows can be lucrative if the weather holds and if the headliners draw crowds. Otherwise the high fees charged by the musicians, often required in advance, and the large initial outlay of cash for technical and staff assistance can spell financial disaster. Some fairs hold dances, as in earlier times, with added admission fees, which contribute to income.

The premium book usually pays for its own printing through advertising and the support of local merchants. Local merchants also usually donate ribbons and trophies used as prizes. These merchants believe that this community service repays them in advertising and community support of their businesses. In effect, local merchants take the place of the landowner-patrons of earlier times.

The state government usually gives some matching funds for some building rehabilitation. But the state government's most important monetary contribution arises in connection with the income from pari-mutuel horse racing. The state donates some of this income to augment the premium money awards to competitors at the county fairs. This pari-mutuel money comes mainly from the Chicago area and provides an example of one of the rare (in the eyes of "downstaters") instances of cooperation between "city" and "downstate."

State and local relations involve more than money. Lobbying and information exchange with state agencies and legislatures occupy the attention of officials of the county fairs. To these ends, concerned fair officials formed the Illinois Association of Agricultural Fairs (IAAF). The IAAF holds an annual meeting at which members hire talent for the midway, give papers, and swap accounts and solutions of problems through the year. In addition the IAAF distributes a newsletter and holds regional meetings.

The legislature and lobbying section of the IAAF pays close attention to legislation, regulation, and political measures emanating from the state government and particularly to those measures that may affect the budgets of fairs. If other agencies try to infringe on funding or county fair prerogatives, the legislative liaison of IAAF lets its membership and the government agency in question know its position. For instance, in the early 1980s the State Fair rather arbitrarily changed its dates for the first time in years. This action put the plans of many county fairs in jeopardy because of the unaccustomed conflict. This was a topic of discussion and letters for months. The dates remained as the state fair had stipulated, but the State Department of Agriculture took note of the issues for the future.

The state, through giving of the premium, or prize, money, keeps a certain watch over the establishment of the more standard payments and categories. The fairs may fund anything they want, but in order to get the government to add funds, they have to construct a convincing case for government assistance to projects (such as preservation of buildings), preferably by combining with some other fairs. Each fair board presents an annual report to the Department of Agriculture with a statement of past expenditures and fiscal plans for the following summer. Then the state officials figure out how much money they will need to allot for premiums.

The state government also establishes rules in which the local agencies acquiesce. These rules concern health inspection, especially of livestock, the fair conduct of harness and Thoroughbred racing, and the prohibition of hard liquor and gambling. This last does not preclude mild games of chance on the midway.

The fair consists of three major administrative areas. Fair board offi-cials who are superintendents take responsibility for the entertainment and midway section, or for the commercial section, or for the judging and exhi-bition section. Commonly, only one person, with the aid of assistants, orga-nizes the first two sections. The judging and exhibition section, however, is subdivided; a main superintendent, with superintendents under him or her, takes charge of each subdivision.

Entertainment at the fair takes place mainly in the grandstand and the carnival. The grandstand fulfills two important functions: it attracts events that command a separate and higher fee than that of the entry gate, and it lures the individuals who are not interested in the judging, exhibits, or mid-way. As mentioned earlier, the grandstand presents a perpetual problem be-cause some acts require their money in advance. The success of the acts de-pends on the acuity of the judgment of the superintendent or the board in choosing in mid-winter what an audience will want to see for one or two nights the following summer.

Success also depends greatly on the weather. One stormy night can wipe out the take from country-western musicians such as Tanya Tucker or Charley Pride and put the fair in debt. Since the advent of television and large recording contracts, the prices for the musicians and their sound sys-tems have risen quite steeply. Sometimes superintendents prefer demolition derbies, motorcycle races, and tractor pulls because these events can be counted on to draw, and although tickets cost less, so does the overhead. The participants also present the advantage of not requiring payment unless they perform. The main costs for those events usually involve only prize money and liability insurance. These expenses come to a good deal less than the $10,000 to $60,000 demanded by country music stars in 1982.

Also included in the grandstand, but sometimes under the aegis of a separate "superintendent of speed," are the horse races. In Illinois, races generally mean harness races with occasional Thoroughbred or "flat" rac-ing included. Racing occupies a peculiar position at the fairs. A strong seg-ment of the population altogether disapproves of horse racing on the fair-grounds because it is said to encourage gambling and lowlife. Advocates of the races point out, however, that as many people find a historical link be-tween racing and county fairs and feel that one would not be complete without the other.[35] Even though not nearly as many folks attend the races these days as used to, advocates believe that patrons of the fair associate the two. And history compels respect in the fairs.

Figure 2.2   Harness racing, Henderson County, Illinois

Entertainment superintendents engage bands, clowns, old-time medicine shows, and magicians, or whatever seems likely to enhance the carnival portion of the fair. These roving entertainers distinctly echo the festive atmosphere of the earlier European fairs. Performing at strategic locations around the fairgrounds, they beguile the tired adults and cranky children and contribute to the unusual atmosphere of the event.

The most important responsibility of the officials in charge of entertainment is arranging for the midway and carnival. Usually a carnival manager will contract with a group of "ride jockeys" (ride operators) and games owners to travel as a unit during the summer. Then the carnival manager negotiates with each fair board for the use of the midway of the fair in question. Most aspirants who want to set up as carnies on the midway must come to an agreement with the carnival manager, although a few local merchants and food vendors sometimes can make separate agreements with the fair office.

Superintendents of the midway and carnival also coordinate charity auctions and local talent shows in the grandstand or elsewhere on the

Figure 2.3   Dan Barth's Medicine Show, Winnebago County, Illinois

grounds. A strong belief exists that civic and charitable organizations are essential to the fair, for it is a community institution.

The commercial and civic section of the fair forms an important component of the attractions. Like the local trading populace of earlier fairs, merchants and exhibitors in these categories attract much interest from passersby. For this reason, they, too, find the fairs beneficial as advertising and for future customer relations. Potential customers spend time at these sections investigating the latest developments in log-cutting machines, child-abuse literature, at-home care products with aloe-vera, beekeeping, pump organs, and the Republican party. The products of this section divide into commercial and civic, and the personnel into traveling and local. Almost all the travelers are in commerce, except for those on the livestock circuit, traveling a regional and seasonal circuit to sell or demonstrate products. They reserve and pay for their spaces about six weeks in advance of the fair.

Local merchants, civic and political groups, and those who set up a food or merchandise booth only for the fair parcel out the local booths among themselves. Often, these people who set up booths only for the fair become known in the town or county for trying new roles. A Ford County exhibitor, Mrs. Denham, said:

> We had a family from this town, the barber and his wife, who ran a caramel corn stand. And they started out with just a little tiny popcorn stand. And they were really the only commercial stand from this area. Then they got into the caramel corn business and they went to other fairs, all around.
>
> I used to run a beauty shop uptown, and this lady lived in back of it. And she still would like to talk of those days. But they were the family from here that really got involved with the commercial end of the fair.

The superintendent or official in charge of the local booths often donates free space to those civic groups that espouse a cause. The space is not in the most desirable location; usually it is far from the grandstand, midway, and center of the commercial action. One man said,

> We try to give space to the ones we feel are the most important to the community or touch the most people. . . . There isn't that many. We have space for people of opposing views—we usually don't give them very good space. We sell the best space and sometimes the civic organizations will buy a better location.

Superintendents of the judging and exhibition section bear responsibility for the primary rationale of the fair. They oversee a large division of the fair in which competitors enter exhibits such as home or domestic arts, livestock, horticulture, or floriculture. Among the most important of their duties is the organization of help for the fair. One of their major roles in accomplishing their task is the appointment of suitable superintendents under them who are responsible for a specific section of the fair within their divisions.

Superintendents watch over all activity in their section at fair time. Carnival folks, commercial and civic exhibitors, and people who show agricultural products all must register and pay a fee. The superintendents oversee registration and prepare the active space of their section. They make a plan showing assignment of that space to particular categories of entries and then they record those entries in books.

The superintendents assemble the ribbons and the trophies. They supervise the judging procedures: they keep the judging moving, record results, and ensure that someone awards the ribbons. They organize the displays or animal pens after all the judging has been completed. Superintendents look after the physical space where animate and inanimate exhibits are housed. Sometimes they also act as chaperons and mentors for the junior exhibitors. During the year, superintendents recommend judges, keep an eye on the maintenance of their buildings, and revise the schedules and categories in the premium books.

Board members choose superintendents (as they themselves are chosen) on the basis of demonstrated commitment, skill, and knowledge and often on the basis of specific familial or community relationships. David Spivak, an official of the Champaign County Fair, said, "We try to get somebody who's involved in that department of the fair or has been involved in showing in that department or who has worked at the fairs, has been concerned about that particular department."

Most superintendents stay on for a long time, exhibiting a reluctance to leave unless they have found and trained a successor. Keith Bergner, a livestock superintendent, said good-humoredly, "I'm training my son-in-law, he's on the board and I can see him, inchin'." Fair workers consider a family connection a natural source for help. These supervisors fulfill their charge of appointing official and unofficial assistants among their neighbors and family. In many of these counties, neighbors are often family. As a rule though, most of these positions, from board member to unofficial assistant, are passed down through and apprenticed for within families. One long-term board member and active volunteer, Steve Johnson, said he had grown up with the fair, working in various sections of the business, and had "married into the shares."

Throughout the arrangement of the fair, family ("blood" kin or fair kin) operates as a major organizing principle. The county fair reinforces the merit of belonging to a family through inherited privilege and through activity. This activity reveals family expectations—if you're related, you help with the work—and the values of connection and participation. Ultimately at least two desirable goals materialize: making and belonging. The plan of the premium book fortifies the concept of family structure through the arrangement of families of categories and classes. The premium book organizes the world into possibilities for creation, into norms and exceptions.

Chapter Three

The Premium Book Categories
Charting Relations of Value

The county fair reinforces the notion that within each cultural context people make categories to separate the things they value from those they do not value.[1] Not everyone values all things in the same degree or manner; people discriminate, usually according to some consistent pattern. Therefore, we (as users, analysts, and audience of things) need to become aware of pattern and thus meaningfulness in each separate context.[2] The divisions in the premium book of the county fair disclose a mental map of the participants in the fair. They signal which things are important enough to be judged in each situation, and they indicate that there is an implied meaning in their arrangement.

In the county fair, the categories appear in the premium book, which provides the basis for organization of judging and exhibition. These small (approximately 8 x 4 inches) paper-covered booklets contain anywhere from 60 to 120 pages of advertisements from local merchants, schedules for events, instructions and rules for entering, lists of categories, and prizes. The premium book is so called because it lists the premiums, or

Figure 3.1   Sandwich Fair premium list, De Kalb County, Illinois

prizes, that is, the ribbons and money paid out for first through fourth, sometimes up to sixth, places in classes such as "Duroc Pigs, Best of Litter" and "Three Jars of Pickled Vegetables." In so doing, the book makes plain the order of the world according to the local participants.

The officials of the fair compose this catalog and keep it current, but they do so in response to and in conjunction with significant community participation and needs. The categories that fairgoers and officials construct "divide up the world" to reinforce and reflect a local useful domestic, social, and economic schema.[3] The continuity of premium book construction provides the basis for judging and exhibition.

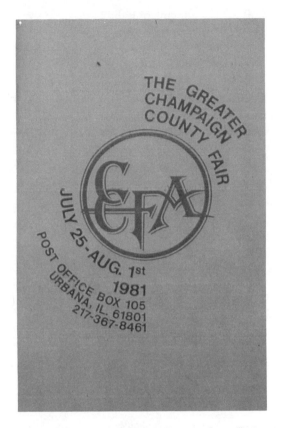

Figure 3.2   Greater Champaign County Fair premium book, Champaign County, Illinois

Livestock, Agriculture, Horticulture, Floriculture, Home or Domestic Arts, and Arts and Crafts constitute the main departments or divisions. Within the Livestock Division, departments of Dairy Cattle, Beef Cattle, Swine, and Sheep occur most commonly. Departments that appear less frequently consist of Dairy Goats, Poultry, Baby Beef, Steers, Horses, and Small Animals (pets, rabbits). Sometimes these last move to a separate division under Domestic Arts, qualifying as hobbies. The agricultural part of the premium book covers seed corn; other grains, such as alfalfa and wheat; grasses; and fruits and vegetables. Sometimes fruits and vegetables are considered separately under a Horticulture Department. Floriculture

General Program of The Fairbury Fair

Wednesday
Family Day

8:00 A.M.	Judging of Exhibits
10:00 A.M.	Rooster Crowing Contest
1:00 P.M.	"Music Through the Years—Act 2"
7:00 P.M.	Band Contest
9:30 P.M.	Illinois Valley Shows on Midway

Thursday

8:00 A.M.	Judging of Exhibits
1:00 P.M.	Thoroughbred Racing
7 & 9 P.M.	Barbara Mandrell
9:30 P.M.	Illinois Valley Shows on Midway

Friday
Kids Day

8:00 A.M.	Judging of Exhibits
1:00 P.M.	Music
1:00 P.M.	Harness Racing
4:30 P.M.	Drawing for Free Prizes
7:45 P.M.	Stock Car Racing (No Time Trials)
9:30 P.M.	Illinois Valley Shows on Midway

Saturday

1:00 P.M.	Music
1:00 P.M.	Harness Racing
7:45 P.M.	Stock Car Racing (No Time Trials)
9:30 P.M.	Illinois Valley Shows on Midway

Sunday

9:00 A.M.	Flea Market
1:00 P.M.	Dog Show
1:00 P.M.	Music
1:00 P.M.	Harness Racing
4:30 P.M.	Micro Mini Tractor Pull
6:00 P.M.	Tractor & Truck Pull

Figure 3.3   Schedule of the Fairbury Fair, Livingston County, Illinois

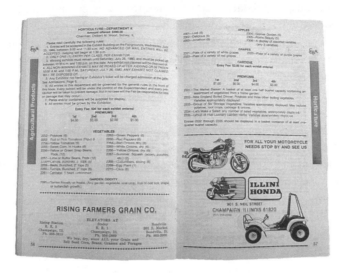

Figure 3.4   Advertisements in the premium book, Champaign County, Illinois

covers flowers. The culinary section encompasses cooked food, such as bread, preserves, candies, and cakes. Several departments, which are kept separate in some fairs and are combined in others, require listing here with all their component parts, since they always turn up in one form or another at the fair: Needlework, Fancywork, Textiles, Crafts, Hobbies, Art, and Fine Art. Some fairs designate a Miscellaneous Department. All fairs include open (adult) and junior (children) shows.

Each fair features some idiosyncratic variation on nomenclature. For instance, one fair may put all its floriculture, fruit, and vegetables under Horticulture. Another fair may call a section foods and nutrition, which yet another one names dairy, apiary, and culinary. Yet another fair may put floriculture, textiles, fine arts, and culinary under Home Economics. Officials often arrange these divisions according to county tradition and according to the availability of personnel to organize the departments. Usually a general superintendent manages each of these divisions, and another group of superintendents looks after each section.

Within the departments appear the names of possible entries, called categories, classes, and classifications, and subsequently their definitions or clarifications. These designations do not remain consistent from fair to fair.

In Illinois, a department called Floriculture, for example, would usually be subdivided into sections, lots, classes, or categories, such as Section I—Specimens, Section II—Arrangements. Under these headings would then come more finely tuned distinctions, which might be termed classes, such as Zinnia, Large, 5 Flowers.

In the paragraphs that follow I list the descriptions for open class (a class that both adults and juniors may enter) livestock. For junior class (open only to entrants under the age of eighteen), the breeds and categories stay the same, but the categories are fewer in number (perhaps four or five under an animal breed as opposed to perhaps fifteen in open or adult class) and the entrants win slightly smaller premiums. In each I give only the most common or representative examples of categories.

Superintendents' Creation of Categories/Community Input

Usually an individual superintendent, although sometimes a steering committee, keeps track of each department. Superintendents control the choice of subdivisions and categories. These people exercise the final decisions about how many and what kind of classes will appear in the premium book, subject to economic constraints and pressure from other members of the county fair community. They maintain records on names of categories and how many people entered in each one. In this fashion, the officials compute how much, if at all, to increase premiums. Available premium monies limit the number of possible entries; presence or absence of interest from participants also limits particular entries.

Superintendents and officials of the fair form categories and take responsibility for keeping them up to date. They accomplish this by tracking what neighbors serve on their dinner tables; what various magazines, catalogs, and breeder's exhibitions feature; what they learn in classes; and what they see in community activities, like church bazaars. They keep up on the demand for certain items in stockyard wholesale markets. And they are not above pirating from other fair books. Mrs. Fennelly, a culinary superintendent and a superintendent of the junior show, said, "Depends on what the kids are interested in . . . we just kind of know what everybody's making. . . . In cooking I just go by what we do at home, and what comes easiest, and you sometimes do what's easiest anymore."

The superintendents try to follow trends, styles, and products that are relevant to the people living within range of the fair. The familiar format of categories presents a background against which changes may be instituted. The people who make the fair (particularly those who decide on the categories in the premium book) act as a kind of bellwether for community taste, as builders and reflectors.

Officials examine existing categories for entries and calculate which are doing well and which are less popular. Sometimes they find that the name of the category is out of date or that the category itself, such as crocheted tatting, is obsolete. Sometimes they notice an omission or a gap in a classification that might draw participants, like zucchini breads.

In order to present up-to-date premium books, superintendents in all departments monitor previous participation in the fair. They maintain records of numbers of entries in each category. Mrs. Hodge, a superintendent in Needlework, like many of her colleagues keeps records of trends in her area; this involves entries in each section from year to year, a map of her space in the exhibition building, and notes to herself: "You can't remember from one year to the next, 'cause the fair only happens once a year." A few visually minded superintendents project an image of the contributions in each class of their departments in their heads; they change categories on the basis of these images of fullness or depletion. If classes have only one or two entries, superintendents usually drop the class. If the classes fill up with ten or twelve entries, they usually split that class into two or more new ones.

Completely new categories that are proposed and published get a two- or three-year chance to gain recognition and popularity. If very few people enter that category during that period, officials substitute new classes. Although only the superintendent can ensure the publication of a new category, community consensus determines its success and maintenance. Individual officials make these decisions only in response to community participation and specific needs. As Jane Turner described:

I was with the committee that helped revise our categories for clothing.

Out of a blue sky, when you don't have anything special, it's hard to think of what the public would demand for categories, whether children's wear or for themselves.

The thing I tried to think was, what I or my friends would sew for the family, so they would have things eligible to enter.

Jane Turner and Mrs. Fennelly, like the other superintendents, are part of the group for whom the categories are created, which gives them a distinct advantage in successfully constructing an attractive set of categories.

People in the community are not timid about making suggestions about new categories by letter, personal conversation, and telephone. Usually superintendents heed these suggestions, although they do not implement every idea they receive. Mrs. Hodge tends to listen more willingly to those people who enter year after year and who make new things every year. "I listen to them—that's the way to improve your county fair, if you listen to what people want." She feels most comfortable attending to a suggestion when three or four people reiterate it. That way probably enough people will enter the new category. She also pays attention to people who possess a greater knowledge of a subdivision, for instance, ceramics. An art teacher she respects has suggested changing the ceramic classifications to "commercial" or "original" molds, rather than using the old classifications of "glazing" or "unique design" in order to avoid definitional problems in judging.

William Beckman, a swine superintendent, puts a suggestion box in the Swine Department, as do the Hawleys, superintendents in the Horticulture Department. The officials at the Sandwich Fair agree that the changing of categories comes through "the interest of individuals, usually. They'll say, we haven't had, and we think this would be a good thing." Paula Hornlein, Culinary superintendent, expanded this statement in a later interview:

> A lot of times it'll come through a request. Somebody'll bring something and say, now, I make this and I don't have a place to show it. So they'll leave that suggestion with us and if we think it's feasible, we'll add that class.

> And if it goes, we'll leave it in the book. If it doesn't, we'll turn around in a year or two and take it out.

She said that sometimes she will adopt a suggestion coming from only one source if it is something she had not thought of or something that has become popular recently.

Mrs. Hornlein's observations indicate that popularity of items influences the selection and survival of categories. Popularity of items often traces back to changes in lifestyle. Some superintendents indicate increased speed and less leisure for the accomplishment of certain tasks as affecting category choices. Breads act as a real barometer of lifestyle changes that inspire entries in the fair. "Cakes are not so strong. Because of the changes in people's lifestyle. You can stick a quickbread in the oven pretty fast. Now yeast you can't make quick," said Paula Hornlein. People with rushed schedules cannot attend to the rising and care of yeast breads.

How particular items keep and show at the fair along with ease or difficulty of production also explains the popularity of a class of entries. The Hawleys described such items with an example: "If it's hard to grow, a poor shower, doesn't last long, especially in hot weather. Solid cabbage keeps pretty decent. We get a lot of cabbages. It depends on the weather or type of year."

Technological changes are sometimes the reason behind the popularity or establishment of a category. The invention of sugar molds brought about a whole new subdivision in decorated cakes.

Exhibitors seem to appreciate change. They want a chance to experiment with new forms. Mrs. Fennelly said, "We like to change around, keep a little interest in." Not enough interest demonstrated in a category through participation spells its demise, except for the instances described later. Conversely, an overabundance of items entered in a class means that another avenue opens up for the community to participate in the formation of categories.

Two ways exist of accomplishing change through excess. One happens through the use of the "any other article" category. "Any other" or "all other," as in Any Other Fruit Pie or All Other Breeds, applies to nearly every department. People often bring items that do not fit into a regular crafts category or flower category but that they want to show. Some people also raise exotic breeds of animals, like Simmental cattle, or unusual plants, like kohlrabi cabbage. They want to exhibit the fruits of their labor and to popularize their breeds and they want to participate.

If the number of entries of one item in an "any other" category becomes extensive, the item will form the nucleus of a new class. One fair added pillows because exhibitors entered thirteen pillows under the category of Any Other Needlework Articles. One woman told me that "any other" is the class used to get ideas for a future class. Judges and superintendents do not like the category because they find it difficult to judge such unlike items as crocheted afghans and petit point chair covers against each other. Still, the class serves as an important catchall, as an encourager of exhibitors, and as a significant straw in the wind.

PREMIUMS

1st	2nd	3rd	4th	5th	6th	7th
$27.00	$25.00	$21.00	$20.00	$18.00	$17.00	$16.00

ANGUS

1 Aged bull
2 Junior yearling bull
3 Summer yearling bull
4 Champion bull.......Trophy
5 Res. Champion bull.......
   Ribbon
6 Pair of bulls, any age
7 2 year heifer and senior
   yearling heifer
8 Early junior yearling heifer
9 Late junior yearling heifer
10 Early summer
   yearling heifer
11 Late summer
   yearling heifer
12 Senior heifer calf
13 Champion Female.........
   Trophy in memory of
   Robert Cresap
14 Res. Ch. Female......Ribbon
15 Pair of females, any age
16 Pair of junior yearlings,
   either sex
17 Pair of summer yearlings or
   younger, either sex
18 Pair, 1 male, 1 female
   (any age)
19 Best three animals, any age,
   either sex
20 Best five animals, any age

HEREFORDS

30 Aged bull
31 Junior yearling bull
32 Summer yearling bull
33 Champion bull.........Trophy
34 Res. Champion bull.......
   Ribbon
35 Pair of bulls, any age
36 2 year heifer and senior
   yearling heifer
37 Early junior yearling heifer
38 Late junior yearling heifer
39 Early summer
   yearling heifer
40 Late summer
   yearling heifer
41 Senior heifer calf
42 Champion Female....Trophy
43 Res. Ch. Female......Ribbon
44 Pair of females, any age
45 Pair of junior yearlings,
   either sex
46 Pair of summer yearlings or
   younger, either sex
47 Pair, 1 male, 1 female (any
   age)
48 Best three animals, any age,
   either sex
49 Best five animals, any age

Figure 3.5 Partial page from the Greater Champaign County Fair premium book, Champaign County, Illinois.

By breaking down any large category into subcategories the community participates and influences category construction in a second tacit way. By the time a class or category gets large enough to divide, distinct patterns of variations have often developed to indicate appropriate lines of subdivision. For instance, within the Culinary Division under "Cookies," one finds "Brownies"; superintendents as a rule regard six to ten brownie entries as the ideal number in a category. That supplies enough to promote competition yet not so many as to make the basis of judging a matter of niggling points; too few entries means the giving of an undeserved premium. If the number of brownie entries rises to twelve or more, the superintendents may decide to divide the major characteristics of brownie production, such as inclusion or exclusion of nuts, into two separate categories. They then hope that the law of averages will push an equal number of participants into either baking brownies with walnuts or leaving them in pristine condition.

In forming classes, superintendents take into consideration the maintenance of consistency of classes so that judges do not have to assess unlike elements. Judging across categories becomes difficult for the judge and unfair to particular entries. Mrs. Hodge said:

> In 1978 we had twelve macrame. So we finally had to split the category because there were so many macrame that it wasn't fair judging twelve because they were different.

> Like now, we have macrame wall-hangings, macrame pot-hangers. . . . You can't really compare pot-hangers to wall-hangings.

The decisions about where to break a category often present difficulties; by which characteristics does one choose to divide? Mrs. Hodge, with the advice of a judge, divided pieced from nonpieced afghans, as encompassing the largest number of cases within. "There really isn't any other way you could do it," she stated, "unless you went to length or sizes." The superintendents try to choose basic construction units that compare in a way meaningful to them, rather than by arbitrary surface characteristics like color. Jane Turner, an exhibitor in Ford County said, "category in sewing doesn't go by fabric, it goes by style or type of garment." But the judge would judge characteristics of each, say, jacket fabric, differently. "So if it's wool," Ms. Turner went on, "the judge looks for finished seams and not if it's double knit." Mrs. Hodge talked about the factors that might make comparison difficult; "I remember there was a beautiful white christening outfit crocheted—now how can you judge that with a sweater? It might have taken a lot more time or it might have been a harder stitch to do."

The same problem comes up in livestock. Judges practically never evaluate unlike breeds against each other, except in the "any other" category. Judges agree that this is a hard category to judge. The superintendents attempt to alleviate the situation by making most categories as discrete as possible in all cases. Whether the category can be divided, however, depends somewhat on the number of entries that fit into a subdivision. In livestock, superintendents consider first breed and then age when creating subdivisions so that size can be more readily compared. Mr. Beckman explained:

> The largest animal usually has the greatest advantage, especially if it's equal in quality, so we narrow the years.

> Some September pigs aren't as valuable as February pigs, so we changed the classes in the fair.

> People used to substitute, illegally, pigs of different months to make them look a lot bigger.

> But a breeder is only as good as his reputation and word gets around.

This problem of discrete categories relates to the problem of defining similar or ambiguous departments. One of the most difficult and often unresolved issues is how to distinguish between art, craft, fine arts, textiles, needlework, and fancy work. The difference in titles and subdivisions detailed earlier in the chapter indicates the ambiguity. Mrs. Hodge told me that someone had suggested to her that any things that have to do with fabric and yarn should go in Textiles, and Fine Arts should contain things like photographs and metals and tole paintings. These ambiguities reveal the difficulty in defining art, especially when similar materials and techniques appear in different categories. The effort to make "art" something unnaturally separate from life becomes evident here.

The community makes its opinions known in the dropping of categories as well as in the adding of them. If very few items have filled a class year after year, then that class stands a good chance of being dropped. Paula Hornlein elaborated the process:

Figure 3.6   Swine exhibition, Henderson County, Illinois

We keep a running account about the number of entries in all of our classes.

If we find that something is beginning to slow down to the point where we won't have only one or two in that class, maybe we'll go for a while and have none, we do cut it out.

We were down to the point where we were getting maybe one or two in the class and they would all be from the same person.

And there just wasn't the show, the competition.

Officials often mention fads or technological innovations as the reasons for dropping a category, just as they influence the addition of categories. Artificial insemination, or AI, has largely obviated the necessity for more than one or two bull or ram classes at most fairs. Sometimes superintendents drop classes to make room in the exhibit space for more popular categories. Categories must change in order to accommodate changes in breeding schedules and climate over the years.

Sometimes the exhibitors influence the category choices from less-than-disinterested motives. For example, most of the officials I interviewed believed that in the Food Division some exhibitors enter the same recipe in two different categories: once under the specifically named category "fudge brownie" and, after adding nuts, a second time under the Any Other Bar Cookie class. They asserted that exhibitors do so in order to win more premium money with the minimum of effort. Some people, they said, will crochet a cape for the crocheted shawl class and then another for the "any other" class. Sometimes they try to cheat outright. For instance, as mentioned earlier, they might lie about the age of an animal, entering an older and thus bigger animal in a younger category because a bigger animal might be judged at the top of its false class. There are rules against these maneuvers, but some people slide by. Thomas Hawley told me, "we used to have a group of midget vegetables . . . but people bring real small ones of a kind instead of midgets. We're taking out that category; they're always trying to pull tricks on you."

Most superintendents and exhibitors alike hold the opinion that those kinds of machinations eventually backfire on those people who practice them. People get a bad reputation, a social and commercial detriment. Frank Weaver, an official of the Sandwich Fair, said:

> People choose categories that are poorly represented in to get premiums the next year. But they can get fooled, because tastes change and everyone might jump at the same time.

> They try to do the same thing in livestock, but they have to be in the age group. If they're being misrepresented, they go to the bottom of the class or get disqualified.

Nearly everyone seems to take a certain pride in at least being knowing enough to see the tricks while deploring their occurrence.

Even though the community forms the basis for category construction, individual superintendents, or the committee made up of officials who depend heavily on data from individual superintendents and their aides, spot new trends, maintain records and traditions, and possess the discretion to make individual judgments concerning unpopular categories. At times superintendents insert categories that result from their own investigations rather than in response to community members' direct or indirect requests. Catalogs of various sorts supply a prolific source of ideas for potentially popular categories, as indicated from this passage by the Hawley family of superintendents of Horticulture for many years:

[Thomas:] We're always ahead of them. We have all the good seed catalogs, and we put it in the book. And we know if we put it in the book, somebody's going to bring it. Maybe not that year, 'cause it's too late, but they'll bring it the following year.

[Mark:] A lot of years, something comes out in the seed catalogs, we're the first ones to ever buy it to see what it looks like, just to get some idea and put it in the book.

Keeping an eye on store offerings and identifying deep-rooted trends that surface in schools and homes and magazine or journal articles occupy a superintendent's attention. In this way, superintendents maintain a vital connection with the active sources of inspiration for their department and for their exhibitors.

Sometimes officials retain unpopular categories. In some cases a superintendent values a category for reasons other than popularity with participants. Some categories continue for interest's sake, for archival reasons, or because they express something about the fair and its ethos.

For instance, "Lard" remains as a category in some fairs, even though it may draw only one entry. Very few people render hog fat themselves these days and use has diminished considerably. But it possesses rarity value, as do canned meats. Paula Hornlein remarked:

We still even have people coming in with a few canned meats. . . . That is a good item for interest. You know, people go through and they really are interested in those canned meats. I think most people wouldn't even recognize what they would look like. People today wouldn't unless they were older farm people who always did that.

So, while we only get maybe three or four to a class, that's a class we leave in because it is becoming such a few and far between thing anymore.

Scarcity or abundance makes a thing interesting or valid for many people. At one fair, superintendent Regina Marshall maintains the category "Illinois History" in the Photographic Division because she connects it with a concept of heritage, important both to people's idea of Illinois and of the county fair, both celebrations of history and a way of life:

We don't get a lot of Historical Illinois any more . . . but at the same time that's kind of important so we haven't really dropped it.

The history of our state, Springfield, the old capital, for instance, it's good for kids to see these things if they can't get down there, things like Lincoln or Salem, sometimes even bridges. . . . I keep them in by my judgment when we make up the book.

Heritage legitimizes many things. The old-time quality of horse racing, acquired because of its long association with county fairs and horse-and-buggy days (rather than with urban race tracks), is losing some of its raffish identity. The distance of history lends enchantment to the view and provides a kind of vacation from the supposed deterioration of contemporary life.

Some fairs feature categories for archival purposes. Someday people might want to know how something is done and to see examples of it. Often, interests return. The Sandwich Fair book of 1880 included macrame. Its popularity returned in the early 1970s. Quilting provides another example of a craft considered passé at one time but which enjoyed a renaissance in the 1970s.[4]

The superintendents make the final decisions for the premium book according to exhibitor activity and personal decision. The economic and democratic process of establishing categories allows people to choose things to enter that they feel worthy of being judged.

Cognitive Maps: The Categories

In most Illinois county fair premium books, superintendents subdivide beef cattle into the most common breeds of Angus, Hereford, and Shorthorn. The most common dairy categories include Holstein, Guernsey, Milking Shorthorn, Jersey, and Brown Swiss. Dorset, Corriedale, Hampshire, Suffolk, Oxford, Shropshire, Montadale, Southdown, and Cheviot breeds show up most often as the classes for sheep. In swine categories, people show Black Polands, Chester Whites, Durocs, Hampshires, Spotted Polands, Yorkshires, Poland Chinas, and Berkshires. All fairs include these typical animals. Most fairs include Cross-bred classes for beef cattle, sheep, and swine. The classes for the smaller animals, such as rabbits and dairy goats, and poultry are arranged in the same fashion as those for the larger animals.

Figure 3.7   Macrame, De Kalb County, Illinois

The highest premiums usually go to the livestock breeders. Participants tell me that the breeders spend more money raising and showing animals than other exhibitors do for entries in their categories. Beef cattle premiums range from about eighteen dollars to twenty-seven dollars (1981) for a blue ribbon, or first place. Dairy cattle premiums tend to equal those of beef cattle. Sheep exhibitors receive premiums smaller than those for beef or dairy cattle. This reflects both that sheep cost less to buy and raise and that they are less crucial to diet and occupation, and thus to the economy in Illinois. Hogs play an important part in the Illinois economy and people like to show them. They grow to maturity very quickly and therefore do not cost as much to raise or buy. Premiums for them tend to equal those for sheep.

The larger premiums for livestock reflect the importance of meat eating in our society.[5] Also, paradoxically, because the animals bear the closest relationship to humans, I think they tend to draw more attention. In addition, beasts are more interesting than tomatoes because they move around. Action compels notice.

After dividing animals by breed, officials institute classes. From fair to fair and breed to breed the observer finds similar classes for livestock. Usually the categories are divided into classes by sex, age, number, and antecedents of the animal.

For instance, the first division for cattle rests between heifers (females) and bulls (males). Dairy farmers, however, emphasize breeding and milk rather than meat. Therefore they place more importance on females, since it is the female who drops calves and gives milk. In beef classes, males are more visible because they grow larger and produce more meat. Beef farmers keep fewer animals for breeding and they slaughter the animals at a younger age. Dairy farmers build their herds over years; a good milker will produce for a long time.

The classes at the fair reflect the importance of females in general in livestock. A preponderance of heifer classes, which include a category for Best Udder in Milk and one for Produce of Dam, as opposed to Get of Sire in the beef classes, highlight this importance. Females produce the offspring. Sometimes fairs encompass both females and males in dairy, but if only one sex is entered, the females will appear in dairy and the males in beef.

Sheep class divisions resemble those of beef and dairy. Ewes tend to be more prominent in sheep showing because, again, breeders build up flocks over the years and the females are the more significant economic factors because they produce lambs. In swine, a boar (male) and a gilt (female) of the same litter often form a class so that judges may examine the breeding quality of the parents. Other group classes include several small pigs of the same litter and their dams or sires.

Age is a factor in creating classes—a two-year-old beef cow at Carroll County in 1980 was one that was calved between January 1, 1978, and August 31, 1978. Superintendents make finely calibrated distinctions in an effort to obtain a consistency of size for each showing. The significant difference in size that can occur within a couple of months makes equitable judging difficult. The casual observer cannot tell if larger size is due to greater age or superior breeding.

"Number" refers to classes characterized by *amount* of animals such as Best Five Animals, Any Age or Pair of Summer Yearlings or Youngster, Either Sex. Often, Pen of Three Rams, Any Age or Flocks of Young Lambs or Flocks of Sheep and various pairs swell the classes. In all livestock group classes, the increased number of classes improve the exhibitors' chances for prizes and exposure. In addition, judging animals in a group helps to indicate presence or lack of uniformity, another criterion for excellence. Many people could breed one outstanding sheep, but breeders also seek reliability of output from a flock, indicated through comparison.

In the separate fairs, different superintendents have instituted various classes for their exhibitors apart from the standard livestock judging classes. The Champaign County Fair puts a steer class in the Beef Department, and a barrow class (market hogs) in the Swine Department. The Ford County Fair also boasts a steer class and a wether (market sheep) class under Sheep. Carroll County features a Quality Steer and Heifer Show, a Beef Carcass Show, and a Calf Scramble and the lead class.

Most of the categories that do not specify breed showcase market animals. These cows, sheep, and pigs have been raised strictly for slaughter and are not judged for their breed qualities at all. Market animals seldom, if ever, are purebreds. Purebred stock furnishes the source for livestock innovations and commercial success. A purebred dairy cow can produce a high-quality calf with specific characteristics if properly mated with the right bull or his seed. Farmers know the cow's and bull's genetic histories. They keep records on their animals' ancestors. They select the animals to mate in order to conceive (with luck) an offspring who will perhaps produce more milk, have a faster conversion of feed to muscle or milk, a sounder udder system, stronger legs, or whatever characteristic breeders deem necessary for the production of a better dairy cow at the time of breeding. Mating of cross-bred or mongrel animals does not offer the controls that does the breeding of animals that have papers testifying to their stock history. It is possible to raise a nonpurebred animal that equals a particular purebred, but cross-bred stock severely limits the breeding capabilities and the predictability of getting an animal with the best characteristics.

The carcass classes allow judging after the animal has been judged on the hoof. Then the animal is slaughtered and the carcass is rejudged for fat, weight, and meat, and then sold at auction. The live market animals are also sold at a county fair livestock auction. The Calf Scramble and lead classes exist primarily to interest the junior exhibitors and to publicize the division or a section of the division (and to emphasize qualities of strength and speed of the animal and familiarity with its habits). The calves entered in the scramble cavort in a separate show prior to the main event, in which

Figure 3.8   Lead and wool clothes class, Carroll County, Illinois

young people try to catch a greased frightened calf or put a halter on it to win a prize.

The lead class emphasizes the exhibitor's showmanship and therefore control of the animal. The exhibitors of dairy animals wear spotless white to point up cleanliness and purity and skill; the exhibitors of sheep, wear clothing that contains wool. One premium book says for those exhibiting sheep:

> The entrant will be judged on mode of dress selected, which must be appropriate, attractive, and lend elegance to the class. Entrant must furnish own costume, made of a wool blend of at least 70 percent wool. . . . sheep used must be registered yearling ewes that have been conditioned, fitted and trained to show at halter.[6]

In all the Illinois fairs I investigated, the departments of the fair followed each other in the same order in the fair book. Livestock usually comes first. After the livestock, set down here in order of their appearance in the book, comes the section on agricultural products and farm products.

Figure 3.9   Grain category, Ford County, Illinois

Considering the importance of corn and soybeans to the economy of the region, the grain classes seem surprisingly small. Corn dominates the premium book in the grain category. Ears of yellow or white corn, popcorn, Indian corn, and calico corn outnumber the rest. The other common grains include oats, rye, wheat, barley, and soybeans, and occasionally, clover seed. Their classes include bundles, bushels, stalks, and flakes. Some fairs put in corn silage (green fodder preserved in a silo) as well as sheaves of those other grains.

In part, fair officials explain the comparative paucity of categories, classes, and entries in grain by citing the commercial grain companies who have taken over much of the responsibility for growing and breeding varieties of grain. Also, farmers who plant hundreds of acres in corn and soybeans do not take much interest in forays into their fields to pick out suitable specimens for show, just as many large-scale beef and hog feeders do not show their animals. The scale of mass production appears to preclude much interest in personal choice or cultivation and subsequent exhibition.

Most grain farmers, aside from a few hobbyists, rest content to let the grain manufacturers test their grain and do not take it further. This is not to say that some people who make a living from agricultural mass production ignore the fair altogether; if they consider themselves part of their community, sometimes they enter other animals or plants or crafts, which they produce on a smaller scale.

Some grain companies, especially in northern Illinois, contribute to the county fair by sponsoring grain shows within grain shows. These companies, like DeKalb Agricultural Research and Jacques Seed Company, offer premiums for the best products resulting from that company's brand of seed. This way the fair acts as an even more direct advertisement and incentive for people growing a particular brand of seed corn. Most farmers sell grain to large corporations rather than to locals, so this show supplies the only real incentive they have to exhibit their grain crops, outside of pure competitive interest, pride, and taste.

Vegetables, fruits, and flowers present a special problem in county fair competition. The date of the fair crucially determines what varieties of produce and flowers will be available for exhibition. Since much produce and most fruits do not ripen until late summer, fairs held earlier in the season make do with a smaller turnout or with judging unripe agricultural products and buds of flowers.

The Ford County Fair, among the first of the season in early July, does not even offer a division for fruits because of its early date. One can, however, as in all the fairs, submit carrots, beets, radishes (red and white), onions (yellow, white, red, and green), cabbage, cauliflower, cucumbers (pickling and slicing), tomatoes, lettuce, kohlrabi, rhubarb (red and green), squash (white, yellow, and zucchini), kale, parsley, potatoes (red and white), beans (wax and green), snow peas, peas, and asparagus.

Champaign County, located one county south in the same region, presents its fair only a week later and offers approximately the same categories for entry but also includes yellow tomatoes, sweet corn, lima beans, butter beans, turnips, green and red peppers, okra, and eggplant. It deletes early crops such as cauliflower, lettuce, and kale.

Fairs occurring later in the season like those at Sandwich and Carroll counties pride themselves on their extensive vegetable displays. Their premium list includes all the above and adds many others.[7] Whereas the Champaign County Fair presents exhibitors with six categories of apples and three of grapes, Carroll and Sandwich fairs, in August and early September, respectively, extend opportunities with pears, peaches, plums, and two kinds of crab apples. Premiums for all the agricultural products run between $2.50 and $4.00 for a blue ribbon.

With the exception of cabbage, cauliflower, kale, and parsley, all vegetables and fruits must be entered in a specified number over one. This relates to internal and external (competitive) comparison; an entry is judged internally for consistency and uniformity as well as externally against its neighbors. Along with the specimens, most fairs invite exhibitors to enter composite exhibits for horticulture; these exhibits are a specialty of all the produce departments. A market basket exhibit in most fairs presents those who wish to use their artistic skills with the opportunity to win from $4.00 to $10.00 for a first prize. The representative Ford County exhibit is described here as an example:

> The market basket—a plain or fancy basket of one-half bushel capacity containing an assortment of vegetables from a garden. The basket should be tipped to resemble horns and should contain a well-balanced assortment of not less than seven or more than ten vegetables.[8]

Other common combination categories listed under this "display" subdivision are Group of Six Storage Vegetables (potatoes, root crops, cabbage, onions), Best Display of Previously Listed Garden Products, a salad bowl display, a New England boiled dinner (potatoes and three other boiling vegetables), and a group of culinary herbs. So, for the fruits and vegetables, as for the Floriculture divisions, the categories divide between specimens and arranged displays of raw materials.

Floriculture classes include potted plants, specimen cut flowers, and bouquets and arrangements. Superintendents limit the account of the potted plant category in some fairs to brief generic descriptions of their horticultural characteristics, such as Grown for Foliage, Grown for Bloom, Succulent, Hanging Basket, Trailing Plant. Other Floriculture departments name a variety of particular potted plants like coleus, ivy, fern, geranium, begonias (varied), palms, African violets, and even terrariums and dish gardens.

The most common flowers for specimens and arrangements are dahlias, gladioli, roses, zinnias, day lilies, petunias, nasturtiums, cosmos, snapdragons, marigolds, and sweet peas. A few fairs include asters and phlox. For arrangements, the titles can be as terse as All Blue or Daisies Predominating, or they can be as florid and descriptive as Anchors Away—Blue and White Flowers—Background from Lake, Sea, River or Ocean, or El Fiesta—Colorful Arrangement with a "South of the Border" Theme, Suitable Container. Carroll County has incorporated a section that features a flower exhibit called "Table Settings." Exhibitors set a table with china,

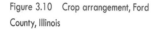

Figure 3.10   Crop arrangement, Ford County, Illinois

glass, silverware, cloths or mats, napkins, and fresh flowers from the exhibitors' gardens. Each of six or seven categories follows a particular theme, such as St. Patrick's Day—4 Place Settings, Luncheon, and Sunday Brunch Buffet.

Every fair includes a division or department for textiles, sometimes called Fine Arts and Textiles. The definitions of what should fit under these headings seem to vary, however. Under Textiles, all entries seem to include needlework of some sort. This usually refers to clothing, infants' paraphernalia, crocheted articles, knit articles, fancywork (embroidery or painting, or one of the two in combination with crocheting, on cloth), pillows, rugs, quilts, afghans, needlework pictures, pillow cases, wall hangings, latch-hook wall hangings, and other miscellaneous handmade textile items.

If included in the Textile Division, crafts (collections, some needle-point, crewel, and cross-stitch items), paintings, drawings, and photography

Figure 3.11   Table setting with flowers, Carroll County, Illinois

surface in a Miscellaneous Department, separate from needlework or fancy-work. In Carroll and Champaign counties, the fair officials have placed painting, illustration, rubout art, ceramics, crafts, holiday theme manufactures, and plaster craft in this category. In fact, superintendents have put anything handmade or hand assembled primarily from inorganic materials in this group. Bread dough art is the only food item in this division.

Some needlework and craft categories are broken down by materials used, some by technique, and some by intended use of the item. Whatever system of separation emerges results partly from the relative importance and popularity of the individual item or class of items in the locale. For instance, in Champaign County, Bridge Cloths or Luncheon Sets is a separate subdivision with such categories as Embroidered Bridge or Luncheon Set; Place Mats (4 napkins); Cross-Stitch Bridge or Luncheon Set (4 napkins); and Embroidered Tablecloths. In Ford County, Lined Garments Only forms a special subdivision under sewing in the Textiles and Fine Arts Department. The individual classes in lined garments are for Ladies' or Girl's Suit, Ladies' or Girl's Coat, Men's or Boy's Suit, Men's or Boy's Coat.

In Carroll County, the fifteen categories of articles possible in ceramics reveal the level of interest and activity in northwest Illinois in studio arts. An Infant's Department under Needlework highlights the popularity and idealization of children, reinforced under Crafts Handmade by Exhibitor. The only category for woodworking in this section is wooden toys. Woodworking occupies four or five categories or even another whole subdivision in other fairs.

The Sandwich Fair, in De Kalb County, features a Needlework Department, a department for art, a separate one for amateur photography, one for collections and ceramics, and still another for crafts. Under Woodworking, it lists subdivisions for furniture (with eighteen categories), veneer inlay, wood turning, wood turning with inlay, and woodworking with handicrafts. All these subsume an average of seven categories. Under Miscellaneous Crafts is listed a category for taxidermy and one for gourd art. Because of the great size of the Sandwich Fair in relation to the others, its proximity to Chicago, its fame, and its end-of-summer date, there are always more categories with greater variation for more people to enter. The proximity to Chicago and to Northern Illinois University also partly explains the interest in handicrafts and studio arts.

Popular literature and memory consistently associate the culinary section with a classic county fair. The section nearly always separates into baked goods (including candy) and canned goods. Those fairs with apiary (beekeeping) or dairy components allow a third subdivision for honey, eggs, butter, and miscellaneous items.

The baked goods section of any fair always depends on the available storage facilities. Officials prohibit cream pies and cakes, since refrigeration is usually impossible. Some spoilage occurs in any case. Breads and rolls, quickbreads and rolls (unyeasted), cakes, decorated cakes, fruit pies, cookies, and candies commonly appear as categories in the premium book. Ford County has started a Cake Mix-Up, Carroll County a special Men's Baking Division (although men may enter anywhere), Sandwich a special division for sugar molds in cake decorating, and Champaign County a pie crust category.

The categories under each division are either general (Covered Fruit Pie) or quite specific (Pineapple Upsidedown Cake). The degree of specificity seems to depend on the particularly popular departments and even categories. The more popular the category, the more specific the details. This allows for more finely calibrated judging.

In the Canned Goods Division the premium books list jellies, jams,

Figure 3.12   Home products, De Kalb County, Illinois

preserves, vegetables, fruits, pickles, and relishes. Ford County (a small fair) does not offer a canned goods category because of lack of recent interest. The other fairs also provide for canned meats, lard, honey, eggs, juice, vinegar, and fruit butters.

Odd Categories

"Odd" categories call attention to themselves. One interesting set of categories within some divisions in every fair present those items that deviate from the usual format and instructions. Superintendents include most of the categories hitherto described on the basis of judging quintessential characteristics of everyday, useful, or recognizable items. Usually when I asked people (judges, exhibitors, officials, patrons) to tell me about the criteria for categories and entries, they selected the norm of everyday life. Some categories, however, do not seem in my observation to count as "serious."

They emphasize the serious points of the fair by their contrasting presence. I found three kinds of "odd" categories. One kind I describe as the category of extremes. The second deliberately breaks rules or locates its contents outside the rules. The third kind of category consists of mutants, accidents, or leftovers. (In the arts or crafts section one finds categories called novelty items, but that usually means something different from an odd category.) Deliberate novelty is art, that is to say, deliberate human construction, as in Novelty Apron, and Unusual Item, under fine arts, or Article Made Something from Nothing.[9] These all appear natural within the context, judged according to similar rules as the other categories. Also, "art" justifies novelty to some extent—thereby connecting definitions with those of the dominant society in this particular division. But some divisions within departments and some categories within divisions rest outside the normal slots for entry.

The first kind of odd category is the category of extremes that contains the champion in each set of livestock breeds and the grand champion in each entire department; the best herdsmen or shepherd award (for neatness of stall, area, display, and general cooperation); Best of Show in Floriculture, Crafts, and Culinary; the memorial awards and trophies; the sweepstakes fruit basket; the floral sweepstakes; or the Grand Champion in Needlework. All departments entice exhibitors with a grand champion or sweepstakes award category at the end of the sections. The Agricultural Produce Department of the Champaign County Fair gives the Dewey Prather Memorial Award. ("The winner of this award is determined by the most places won by an Exhibitor in this department. This person's name shall be permanently inscribed on the Dewey Prather Memorial Plaque.")[10] The Sandwich Fair presents Grand Champion Canner and Grand Champion Baker awards. For hobbies, in Carroll County, "a special award will be presented to the 'Best of Show,'" and "a Sweepstakes ribbon will be awarded to the exhibitor winning the most prize money."[11] In Ford County, "the exhibitor winning the most Blue Ribbons in Department Q [i.e., Miscellaneous—art, collections, crafts, photography] will be presented with a special gift by the Ford County Fair Board."[12]

These sweepstakes or champion categories furnish an incentive for exhibitors to enter a great many items in a great many classes, thus swelling exhibits and income. They also nourish the need for a special focus or highlight, an extreme of excitement and achievement that can be reached by a member of the exhibiting community. All of these headings

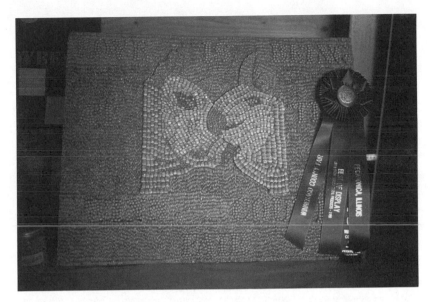

Figure 3.13   Best of display (five grains arranged in design on a board), Winnebago County, Illinois

intensify existing sections. They highlight the regular judging classes by singling out and rewarding those who do best in as many of those classes as possible. These "odd" categories feature the exaggeration of the quintessential, that is, Best Over-all Hand-Knit Article, or Grand Champion Steer over All Breeds; this is a category for excess.

In the second odd category, the deliberate breaking of rules, or the location of categories outside the rules, often provides the locus for the trial of new possibilities or ideas. For instance, one of the generally established rules of most fairs demands that items entered in the domestic crafts and arts sections must be homemade. And in most cases, entrants make cakes from scratch; construct crafts from original designs, not kits; and embroider and knit by hand. Superintendents have permitted special divisions, however, for things like Box-Cake-Mix-Up (combining different mixes plus the baker's own additions); machine knitting, which officials highlight as separate—"Knitting (no machine knit except where stated)"; and needlepoint kits, a special category in some fairs called Design Already Worked —Only Background by Exhibitor. These categories allow room for the increasing number of people who wish to exhibit combined homemade and prepackaged items. Officials maintain the principle of creation but recognize new lifestyles that may eventually be reflected as an accepted part of the fair. At this time, these "odd" divisions emphasize the norm.

Similarly the livestock section emphasizes purebred animals for showing at the fair. The market classes and lead classes, however, acknowledge the growing importance of other commercial dimensions of livestock raising, such as the mass feeding of animals for slaughter. Carcass classes fulfill the same function as the market classes and lead classes.

The Children's Parade and the President's Cookie Jar break rules, since they are multimedia experiences. In the Children's Parade, very young children dress up and exhibit using a variety of media, and in the President's Cookie Jar, people bake for judging on criteria different from those used in the judging of ordinary baking or crafts. The President's Cookie Jar is a specially decorated container of varied cookies that officials later donate to charity. In this cookie category, officials permit more than one type of cookie to be submitted, a deviation from judging the essence of chocolate chip cookie or a butter cookie: one cookie, one category.

At the Sandwich Fair, the subdivisions for the Art of Bonsai, the Floating Rose in a Bowl, the pumpkin show, and the figure or scene made from vegetables provide further examples of deliberately constructed deviations from ordinary categories. The Art of Bonsai was held on Sunday, apart from the ordinary judging days of the fair. It consists of plants, like the rest of the department of Floriculture in which it finds itself, but I saw it as a different type ("little trees"—that is, not specimens or arrangements). It might eventually become part of the categories of the fair, but at this time it is anomalous.[13] The fair accepts the bonsai into the offerings but it does not absorb bonsai into the structure. The Floating Rose in a Bowl, the pumpkin show (carved, decorated, or painted pumpkins), and the vegetable pictures again can be defined as artificial manipulation of nature forms. Of course, that statement also describes the growing and breeding of any vegetables and animals. These items, however, are not vegetables and they are not crafts.

All of these entries cross categories. They appear at interstices where innovation and enlightenment often occur. They all permit a different age group to participate, and they combine elements of ordinary judging in an exaggerated or unusual fashion. They provide new juxtapositions of familiar forms with which people can break out of routine and into new perceptions.

The last two characteristics form important components of the cate-

Figure 3.14   Decorated pumpkins: Miss Piggy, De Kalb County, Illinois

gories that act as play or parody.[14] Accidents, mutants, and leftovers compose this third group. Almost all of these items show up in the sections dealing with garden or farm produce. People definitely considered these "outside" the regular categories. In the midst of lists of potatoes (red chieftain, peck), tomatoes (oxheart, red, 1/2 peck), and squash (large, dark green, 3) materialize categories like largest potato by weight, largest onion, tomato, pumpkin, and so on. Some fairs add Most Odd Potato. Other fairs provide for the tallest stalk of corn, the largest ear of corn, the most odd-shaped ear of corn, and the largest asparagus stalk. In all of these cases, people consider these categories as displays of nondeliberate effort, or efforts judged apart from the ordinary business of growing. Some fairs, like the Sandwich and Champaign fairs, have a special division called Garden Novelties, which the premium book describes as any garden novelties—such as yard-long beans, snake cucumbers (very long cucumbers that curl like a snake), and so on—not listed in the book. A subdivision of Garden Novelties is called Garden Freaks, described as "any vegetable, vine crop, fruit of odd size, shape, or outlandish growth."[15] The very words indicate norms and departure from those norms.

In crafts at the Sandwich Fair, this acknowledgment of the outlandish

Figure 3.15   Vegetable display,
De Kalb County, Illinois

continues in the Ceramics Division, where a category called Ceramics (other than Glaze or Stain), subtitled "Goofs, Misformed Pieces, and Bad Casts, Overfiring, Any Article" attracts exhibitors.[16] This category reinforces the notion of chance or accident producing an admissible or exhibitable piece. Officials allow leftovers in the miscellaneous crafts section, where Novelty Item, Made from Scraps makes a class. The word *novelty* here indicates that it is not usual.

These categories all comment on the ordinary categories. They point up the regulars by showing the irregulars. People agree that these are not "serious" categories. They are not being judged by the same criteria that apply to the standard categories. The "fun" categories gently push the boundaries outward.

The fairs make no room for violent change, but they do accommodate originality, eccentricity, and alteration. Exhibitors can choose to conform

Figure 3.16   Novelty art: nylon-stocking figure in a bottle, Ford County, Illinois

or rebel. The two fairs with the largest number of entries also entertain the largest number of "play" categories. Perhaps only the institutions with an overabundance of participation can afford to experiment with the foundations of their success.

The odd categories embrace extremes, the unusual or fantastic. They parody the ordinary categories, much as in some ways the carnival parodies the agricultural section or domestic life. They stand in the same relation to the ordinary categories that the night and weekend do to the day and week. These categories comment on and release the participants from the distilled concentration and the simulation of the business of everyday life. They are not included in every department or in the same department of every fair. But they do exist as punctuation in some cases and somewhere in every fair. Their existence sketches the judging criteria and the deviation from that criteria. In the making of categories, people reach a consensus of what constitutes appropriate entries, but they allow room on the margins for experimentation and play.

For all of these normal and odd categories, the superintendents, fair officers, and participating exhibitors have evolved what I term a philosophy of choice. Underlying values of gender, age, professionalism, and consistency, emerge through the classification. Definitions of phenomena affect the selection of categories.

Age, gender, and professionalism produce factors of division in category construction. Age has been described previously as a criterion of category separation. There are sections for juniors and adults. Juniors can choose to compete with adults, but they also have their own, inviolable, section, where they compete only with their peers. This presumes developmental progress in the fairs. "Some of these had to be broken by age, because the kids were competing eight years against eighteen year olds, and that's not fair," said Mrs. Fennelly.

Gender Distinctions

Gender produces interesting divisions in some fairs. As with age, if officials specify a category for a certain gender, only members of that gender may enter. No stated rules stop either gender from entering categories unspecified by sex. Gender is not intrinsically attached to farm and agricultural produce. Still, custom, not law, precludes one sex or another from entering any of these nongender-specified sections. Women enter men's categories with less problem because males have culturally higher status and also apparently lose their gender identity more easily.

For instance, although men and boys traditionally have raised and shown livestock, especially larger livestock, like cattle, more and more women apparently have taken to exhibiting livestock in recent years. They do very well in their classes and seem to feel little self-consciousness about showing their animals. Women do not receive special encouragement to enter in these categories.

There are other categories scattered throughout the premium book that do not specify gender but in which one or the other sex enters more often. Exhibitors and officials seem to consider woodworking and metalcraft more masculine, although women enter; they consider knitting and embroidery more feminine. Rug making is considered a province of both sexes.

In the departments and divisions in which women commonly have held sway, men seemingly have felt more reluctance to exhibit. They require enticement with special subdivisions like the one in the plants and flowers section in one fair: "The Masculine Touch, Arranged and Exhibited by a Man."[17] Other categories do not preclude men from entering. They often enter in the Roses subdivision, in particular. But flower arranging seems to hold certain feminine, and thus devalued, connotations; only an occasional courageous and secure man enters in the regular flower-arranging sections.

Another fair arranges a Men's Baking subdivision. Men enter in almost all of the regular culinary departments, but not in noticeable numbers. Men seem to regard most food categories as female. Louis Olmert, a swine exhibitor, spoke for men in cooking:

> For men, the cooking is a hobby, and [they develop] pride to beat a woman in cooking, but they just took it up as a hobby.

> And then they found out they could enter in there and maybe there's a woman who's won out here at the county fair for years, they want to come out here and put something in there, take a chance on maybe coming out ahead.

There are no special "Ladies'" or "Women's" categories in any of the fairs. The traditional structure of the categories reinforces gender distinctions but retains enough flexibility to allow the possibility of change. As in the introduction of technology into food and clothing production, such as the Box-Cake-Mix-Up and machine knitting, the items that highlight the norm also possibly illuminate the way of alteration.

Professional and Amateur

Livestock superintendents do not appear to believe in dividing the professional breeders from the hobby breeders. Those divisions are not always stated or clear in those sections. In fact, for most livestock breeders, their hobbies are their professions. Most breeders devote their primary attention to this occupation; animals require a lot of care. The expenses involved also ensure that most breeders will try to make money where they can.

The same almost always holds true of agricultural products. Officials address the possible amateur-professional problem by an insistence that the produce be grown by the exhibitor or on the exhibitor's own land. Here they emphasize a preference for the local over the outlander. They want participants to be committed to the area and to the process through their own efforts or through their land, an extension of themselves. What entrants later do with that produce, as with the livestock, is of no concern to the fair.

Still, "purely commercial producers of hybrid seed corn are excluded."[18] Again, personal commitment and the chance to start with equal opportunities and resources for competition underlie the rules. Also, this provision indicates the prevalence of corn and bean agribusiness in this region; big business has found crops more lucrative than beasts here, and therefore the fair officials encourage professional livestock breeders whereas they would not encourage commercial seed corn producers. Certain departments of some county fairs even more strictly preserve the gulf between professional and amateur.

Professional and amateur distinctions become important when the standards might diverge. This is an issue in Floriculture, and in the Art, Culinary, and Needlework departments. Opinion has it that professionals in these areas possess a possible unfair advantage in expertise and a different concept in execution. Fair officials do not exclude professionals from participation in most cases; they merely give them separate categories to enter, thus putting them in their place. One fair notes that "whenever amateur is listed, it refers to the ability and experience of the person and not to the entry," thus preserving the distinction between resources and value judgments. The Greater Champaign County Fair fairbook defines *amateur* as "a person who earns less than half their income in the area of Art."[19] Again, here, the officials carefully do not evaluate the final product so much as try to ensure that people begin equitably. Those who earn their income at an occupation presumably spend more time and research at their pursuits and also develop a helpful professional network.

The larger the fair, the more concern officials demonstrate in distinguishing between amateur and professional. In Carroll County, in the Floriculture Department, it is stated that "No professional florist or person engaged in growing or arranging flowers for profit is eligible to compete for premiums in this department." Other departments simply make a distinction between professional, instructor, and amateur. In Fine Arts, where the rules permit professionals, they enter a special subdivision called Instructor class. In Sandwich Fair, the Culinary Division includes amateurs' and professionals' specialty cake categories for decorated cakes.[20]

The Sandwich Fair divides clothing categories into "professional" and "nonprofessional." Professionals are defined as "those who consistently sew for others for a monetary gain." In the Sandwich Fair's Art Department, officials define professionals as "those who have one or more degrees in art, who do work for livelihood or consistently sell their paintings, teach others for a fee, maintain a studio, or those who consider art their career." They, too, enter special classes if they fit this definition: "An amateur is one who does art as a pastime, has no degree in art, receives no fee for instructions, and exhibits primarily for pleasure of showing work." In a few departments, amateurs and professionals may enter in the same classes. In Photography, as in Floriculture, they are excluded from entry. Antique dealers may not exhibit in collections and ceramics sections, nor may those selling crafts at the Sandwich Fair enter. Of course, sometimes amateur flower arrangers, rose breeders, or cake decorators become professionals after they exhibit for a time at the fair, win prizes, find their services in demand, and begin to make a living at what began perhaps as a hobby.[21]

Whereas in the Livestock and Crop Growing departments professionalism, contrasted with pure commercialism, is considered part of regular exhibiting, in others professional activity constitutes an unfair advantage. Categories or departments in which exhibitors have a great deal of control over the construction of their entries (unlike livestock or produce, which depends on nature for a certain amount of the result) are more rigorously compartmentalized. The issue of how much money is derived from art or constructed products sparks concern among amateur entrants, who feel they lack something that "professionals" or "artists" have and to which they presumably have no access. People do not assume such a gulf in the growing or raising of farm-related things; they accept the need for special equipment and practice if they are serious. They feel they can obtain these with money and time. They do not often seem to need the professional/amateur distinctions for the baking of bread and the sewing of quilts, activities that people see as part of their natural domain, yet as difficult to execute as a decorated cake or a hand-built pot. But for more clearly artificial constructions, people seem in some cases to feel the need for distinctions. Money and the mystique of art are the defining factors here. Domestic life, farm life, becomes the familiar, unmarked way of life. Art becomes the marked, separated category for something outside everyday life. The value system that emerges forms a part of the system by which people make sense of their world.

Purebred and Homemade

The ideal of value combines purebred and homemade. The dominant categories emphasize these qualities as the accepted basis for choice. Alternative categories, such as the "biggest" or the "weirdest," clearly locate themselves out of the mainstream; they embody values that are contrary to the ethos of the fair. The standards here encompass control over nature, non-mixing of categories, and painstaking effort at producing a special kind of animal.

In the same way, officials iterate community issues of control, quality, and personal labor as they insist on items being home grown ("All exhibits must be grown by the exhibitor," "All entries of natural flowers must be owned and grown by exhibitor," "Exhibitor must be bona fide owner and raiser of fruit and vegetables exhibited")[22] or homemade, produced by the exhibitor. Kits, or partial kits, are admitted—sometimes tacitly—in some sections of craft or needlework departments. Some superintendents believe in the expedience of kits. They feel that kits encourage potential exhibitors to participate in some form in the making of things, and a minority believe that kits are better because they produce less messy and more polished results. But for the most part, all believe that the fair is the place to exhibit personal involvement with the creation of an object, with whatever degree of innovation on the part of an exhibitor; thus, the injunctions "All articles must be made entirely by the exhibitor," "All work must be the original work of the entrant," "No commercial mixes may be used in any of the baking or candy categories," and "No article may be purchased in a store, imported from a foreign country, made in a factory, or borrowed."[23] Officials prohibit paint-by-number kits, because, they say, "creativity is usually judged higher than the kits," thus reiterating the premium on homemade items.

The categories for market animals and the occasional Cake Mix and Extra Ingredients Added by Exhibitor or Machine-Knit Afghans offer opportunities for change. But the issue addressing originality, homemade or home-raised items, and purebred livestock is twofold. One, the fair provides philosophical and methodological alternatives to the machine age, even though the fair sponsors the latest machines elsewhere in the fair. The fair also sponsors a reminder of roots, the underpinnings of any sort of innovation, creativity, or change.

The categories emphasizing homemade characteristics provide alternatives to current economic or social considerations. The fair categories actually are old-fashioned and progressive simultaneously. They require procedures and values that have gone by the board in this era of convenience foods and kits, but at the same time they demonstrate the latest developments in design techniques, visual style, nutrition, and farming techniques.[24] These categories contain essential ideas for the way we live in the world (a cultural gene pool) and provide new models for thought even though they are "old-fashioned" nontechnological categories. They are not mere repositories in a museum sense of quaint antiquarian customs but storehouses of necessary knowledge and methods that not only might be needed again some day but that combine this minute with unlikely mates and new developments to produce illuminations of new paths.[25]

In the same way, the fair sets up a value system in part contradistinction to that embodied by the current commercial and time-constrained preoccupations of this era. Although the fair is a source for commercial and technological development, it emphasizes personal, participatory modes more than mass-market values. The fair tells participants that identifiable core elements construct a stable base for innovation and creativity, like cores in the physical layout. The modes of purebred and homemade require more time and effort than the mass production of animals or use of ready-made kits, but they bring about solid changes through a combination of recognizable elements regrouped or permuted to meet an individual situation. Sometimes they form new recognizable bases (referring to a history) that can be used to innovate again.

Chapter Four

"A Good Judge"
The Ritual of Evaluation

*A good judge is one that will be sure and tell
them why they picked the winner. I think that
is important, that they don't just say, well, this
is a winner. If they can justify why they picked
this person, then they're going to have to put a
little more effort into it, 'cause there's going to
be a lot of people out there being critical of
their explanation.*

David Spivak, Champaign County Fair

People create their entries according to and in response to the standards and aesthetic criteria expressed by the judge and community who evaluate their work. Those standards get into the minds of the makers and raisers through the ritual performance of exhibition and evaluation at the county fair.[1] This ritual performance allows community values to emerge through action as well as through expressed standards. As David Spivak's statement illustrates, the judging process involves a process of responsiveness, accountability, and location of self in community.

The Judges

The superintendents of departments choose the judges. If the fair's board acts as the agent for the final selection of judges, it selects them only after extensive consultation with the superintendents. Most superintendents, however, usually choose their own judges because they know their own field well. A former president of the Ford County Fair summed it up: "Going back to the selection of judges, during my tenure, I always left it up to the superintendent of each class, because who in the world would know better than they did?"

Superintendents find suitable judges in various ways. Usually they locate personnel through some kind of direct personal or professional experience. Some judges receive formal training from Agricultural Extension agencies, some through university affiliation, and some through professional organizations like craft guilds or breeders' associations. Some judges hold university appointments in Domestic Science or Animal Science programs. Others derive their experience from their positions in the profession; they breed animals, show photographs, sort seed types. A few county fair judges may gain their whole livelihood from judging, but the greater number both judge at fairs and follow their related professions.

A Livestock Division superintendent might know of a good judge through bigger fairs, like the state fair, through county fairs far from home, through livestock sales or breeders' shows, or just through daily work and contact with livestock events. In other parts of the fair, superintendents follow the same pattern in discovering judges. Their own interests that led them to their positions as superintendents in the first place also lead them to circumstances in which they will find good judges. Classes; craft shops; discussions with home economists, Home Extension advisers, and teachers; and participation in professional activities constitute a pool for the selection of potential judges. Thomas Hawley, a horticultural superintendent, described the various sources for locating judges in horticulture: "We have one judge who is qualified to judge the hybrid seed corn. He worked with DeKalb Ag." Mark Hawley, his son, added, "I used to have one that ran a grocery store, two great big grocery stores, and he bought all the produce for 'em. Our fruit judge has an orchard. The lady that judges your juniors, she had judged your other 4-H fairs and things of that sort. And our herb judge, they operate an herb store."

Superintendents and fair board members agree that apart from direct contact, they also choose judges by word of mouth or reputation. Agriculturalists often build commercial transactions on reputation so it looms large in the world connected with county fairs. One must to a certain extent trust breeders, growers, bakers (that is, professional colleagues), and one's social relationships. Sometimes a judge chosen by word of mouth is more desirable than one's professional contacts because word of mouth implies a greater social detachment. A Sheep Division superintendent, Wendell Brown, said:

> I think it's by word of mouth more than anything. You hear of different judges that are *good* and from there you choose three or four that you feel are well-qualified.

> This gets to be a problem because you would like to get someone out, away, that is not associated with the people who are showing the animals. It's easier.

Many superintendents agree on the importance of selecting a judge who does not have friends showing at the fair or who will not recognize friends' work.

In a circumscribed region, however, it is impossible always to use judges who are unacquainted with the exhibitors. For one thing, the fairs can afford to pay only limited reimbursement for travel, and the fee for judging might not be worth a judge's travel time. Officials pay judges in most fairs anything from merely nominal fees up to one hundred dollars for an engagement that usually lasts not more than two days.

Good judges are often asked to return year after year. Superintendents and exhibitors (the ones who win) say, "Why change just for the sake of changing?" and "When we get a good judge we keep him." Sam Rogers, Sheep superintendent, described his preference in this matter: "It's customary to have them at least two years in a row. It's kind of a compliment to them that you like them and you'd like to have 'em back for at least one year."

The average attitude, however, appears to be that while a good judge should be retained, some change is required for the sake of interest and fairness. Even the winners concede that some change is necessary. Officials say one reason that entrants like change is because a particular judge often emphasizes particular things. John Bergner started to discuss the issue by saying, "Well, you get a little different idea if you get a different judge, his ideas. This way, you just kinda change that every two years." Al Gordon, currently on the board of the Ford County Fair, continued the thought: "Another thing is, anyone who shows livestock knows, they might win at one fair and lose at the next one. So, if you don't have a different judge once in a while. . . . you don't want them to get in a rut." John Bergner interjected: "You get a lot of partiality, too." And Al Gordon finished: "Sometimes you get a guy that don't like the judge and if you have the same one all the time, he's going to stay home."

Participation is the goal here. Fair officials strive to attract exhibitors in livestock and all the other sections. There is a reluctance to exhibit if they feel the judge is always likely to be "political"—partial or corrupt, in the language of the region. As Ed Luseby, a livestock judge and an Animal Science professor at the University of Illinois said:

> If I'm going to do it in a political way, I just don't care to do it, because you're not proving anything.

> If I was a breeder, the ideal thing would be to have the champion bull at Denver, at the Stock Show. . . . you know I'd like to do it honestly but sometimes it's done political.

> In other words, this fellow says "you know, I know this fellow likes my kind of bull because he bred some of these kind of cattle, they go back to the family of cattle that HE had and if I get that judge, he, he KNOWS that I've got his family of cattle and he KNOWS I paid him a lot of money for this particular one and you know, he wants me to promote HIS cattle and so if I get that fellow to judge animals that came of HIS breeding, he's going to put them up." And that becomes political, which is not absolutely one hundred percent right.

> So you have to have an unbiased opinion.

The exhibiting community does not generally make suggestions as to which judges should be hired. They frequently make their influence felt, however, in the termination of judges. If a sufficient number of exhibitors complain about the judging, then the judge may be removed after the fair. As Mrs. Elaine Hawley, a horticultural superintendent, said, "We don't have very many complaining. But if a lot of them *would* complain, then we'd consider getting another judge." Almost all superintendents agree that if the exhibitors were unhappy, the judge would be reviewed and dismissed, and a new judge hired. The structure of the fair and the mores of those running the fair allow interested participants from the county the opportunity to involve themselves in some of the crucial decision making.

County fair rules and custom designate the judge as the final arbiter during the judging and usually during the fair. While a significant number of complaints about the same judge will practically ensure a new judge for the following year, usually the present year's decisions are incontrovertible. The fair patrons do have the satisfaction of knowing that their wishes will be heeded in the future, but the current fair may not be disrupted. The disgruntled exhibitor might reach a final court of appeal at the fair office. Complainants often arrive at the fair office and state their grievance. If some obvious and gross inequity has been perpetrated, the fair officials will try to rectify the situation as soon as possible. If, on the other hand, and as is often the case, a person is merely dissatisfied, he or she will be required to begin a long and expensive complaint procedure, which is in fact rarely invoked.

Superintendents, officials, and exhibitors cite four or five criteria for determining a good judge, just as they do for determining good categories and as the judges and exhibitors do for determining a good entry. One important characteristic requires that the judge should beget as few complaints as possible, thus reinforcing an objective of social harmony. Everyone agrees on the impossibility of pleasing everyone; some will always complain. But some judges approximate community consensus better than do others. Some judges' decisions, even while not approximating community consensus, carry more weight than others' do. This means the judge conveys knowledge, confidence, fairness, and understanding of the fair community's values in order to forestall as much discontent as possible.

The verbal performance of the judge accentuates many of these qualities. For the fairs that have any kind of open judging attended by the public, an articulate judge becomes an absolute necessity. Even superintendents with closed judging in their sections demand some ability on the part of the judge to explain his or her decision, either in writing on the exhibitor's entry cards or to the superintendents so they may explain later to the exhibitors the rationale for the judge's actions.

Superintendents find this quality particularly essential for those judging 4-H and juniors, because they are concerned that the fair be a learning experience for children. They want children to understand why one item or animal rated higher than another. This both helps the children change elements that are considered wrong and makes them (and their parents) aware that the judge's decisions are not completely arbitrary.

Judges demonstrate their good faith and skill in their judging presentation. If they demonstrate competence, they gain the trust of the audience. The exhibitors enjoy technical knowledge and have a personal stake in the explanation; therefore they pay special attention to the judge. The casual fairgoers often have little knowledge and thus require an interesting, coherent explanation. The judge must accommodate both audiences in domestic and horticultural arts as well as in livestock judging. A judge creates a kind of public persona in order to communicate what is necessary and to whom it is necessary. The judge works under public scrutiny and answers to an audience, directly or indirectly. "Because we *are* judging in front of people, it does have to be somebody that can take this, can judge and listen to the criticisms and the comments on her judging and be able to stand up to all of that at the same time," remarked Paula Hornlein of home arts judging. She indicates the responsiveness and the degree of audience interaction needed by the judges for their performance.

The judges must know the field. While they are judging other people's work, people judge the judge's own performance. Those judged sometimes possess as much knowledge as does the judge. The judge is the authority for the day but is working under the eye of the authorities. One superintendent was very distressed that the judge in one department exhibited ignorance of many of the techniques in the section. This superintendent said to me, "But I couldn't say anything, she was the *judge*." This judge was not asked back.

A good, competent judge examines the skills and results in each section for which he or she is responsible. The superintendents want the judges to have had extensive experience with the products. This means knowing the stitches in all of the needlework examples, being familiar with the properties of wood, ceramics, metals, or different frostings for cakes, and types of jellies, and the proper look of each vegetable on the premium book list.

Knowing the field means also that judges keep up with the latest developments in their field. Criteria and methods change constantly, just as the categories do. The judges have to be a part of that dynamic or lose their audience. When one culinary judge felt she did not have sufficient familiarity with sugar molds for cake decorating, she requested that a specialist be added. If she had needed more than one specialist, her appeal probably would have dimmed.

Judging technique determines competent judges. Some exhibitors in Ford County were upset one year when the judge in one section made a

Figure 4.1   Chocolate judging, Ford County, Illinois

very perfunctory tour of the exhibits. They told me that a judge should take time enough to examine the entry with some attention, care, and concern for detail. Thus judges make their performance match the effort of the creators. Similarly, in food, Paula Hornlein said,

> A good judge can pace herself. If she's judging chocolate, she's going to judge so much of that and then she's going to something else and change her taste for a while. Because, having done a fair amount of food judging, if you're not careful in what order you judge things, you can get into a problem as far as your taste buds are concerned.

Versatility characterizes a good judge. A judge who knows his or her particular field thoroughly can judge different breeds of dairy cattle, different fabrics in sewing, or different varieties of seed corn.

The last issue in what determines a good judge concerns his or her background. Some conflict arises in the choice between judges who have book, or theoretical, learning and those who have practiced what they judge. Most officials and patrons prefer a person with practical experience

Figure 4.2   A finished garment, Ford County, Illinois

along with formal education. This assumes that the judges have been in the same position as the exhibitors but that they also know the latest developments through classes or private study. Robert Edwards, a cattle superintendent, like so many of his fellow superintendents, favors someone, university-trained or not, who has had practical experience in the field they are judging:

> I usually go by somebody that has either shown there and isn't showing there anymore that's an older fella, or try and get somebody that I've shown against like at State Fair.

> If you show cattle and have shown them all your life, you know yourself what the traits of the good animal are, what you're looking for, everything that's involved in it.

Community members often perceive university faculty as interested only in theory or book ideas that have no real application to the issues of everyday life. The exhibitors and superintendents alike want someone who understands the problems of the exhibitor, who has a stake in the same kind of production of entries as those who show, and who is not removed from the consensus of the community.

The Exhibitors

Physical preparation by exhibitors for this judging process can commence as much as a year in advance or as little as the night before entries are due at the fair. In the case of livestock, animal raisers sometimes have to arrange breeding schedules according to fair dates. Such arrangements can entail quite a bit of advance planning. For instance, dairy cows show best when they are in milk and when they distend their udders to feed calves. Dr. J. M. Dodd, Dairy Science professor and judge, said, "If everything worked in the barn the way it does on paper, then you'd be fine. To look good in a show, you have to plan way in advance. It takes some manipulating." Gestation cycles play an important part in determining whether one shows February or September pigs, yearlings or two-year-old calves. Exhibitors need a certain amount of time to train their animals for the show ring. The animals must learn how to walk and stand and be set up. Halter-breaking any animal except pigs takes some time. Time is not much help, I was told, in showing pigs. Apparently all the exhibitor can do is try to get to know them, learn to use a swine prod, and hope for the best.

The preparations necessary for showing livestock involve choosing a show string of animals about two months before the fair and then watching and training them carefully. Sam Rogers, a sheep breeder, said,

> They can go off feed, go downhill, or one blossoms or a pastern could break.

> Then around July 4 for a July 23 fair you start washing them when you've made your final selection. Put 'em in a stand with water, soap, and a hose, their head's in a frame. . . . we have a power washer, it does a pretty good job—it's high pressure.

All animals need to spend at least a week or two getting cleaned up for the fair and having special care taken of them before exhibition time. All of them have the fields or barns washed off them, often a special diet prepared, and a regimen of brushing instituted.

Figure 4.3   Sheep grooming, De Kalb County, Illinois

Shortly before the fair begins, exhibitors enter a rigorous phase of preparation of their animals. Robert Edwards, who shows dairy cattle, embarks on a program of trimming and clipping a day or two prior to the fair to get his animals ready for show.

> Clip all the hooves and fit 'em and size 'em up [making sure the hooves are evenly planed] so they walk better on 'em.

> And when you clip, you clip all the hair off the heads and trim the tails and blend in the shoulders.

> A good groomsman gets anywhere from twenty-five to thirty dollars a cow.

> I groom them myself.

Beef cattle and sheep flourish under the same sort of cosmetic preparation. Livestock exhibitors clip or shear the animals in certain patterns consonant with the current criteria used in judging. They rat the tails of beef animals

Figure 4.4   Cattle grooming,
Waukesha County, Wisconsin

and spray them with hair spray, and tie a knot in the bottom, or they might
even braid them. Exhibitors used to block and card sheep's wool into a
boxy shape and curl a steer's hide. Now they tend to shear the animals a little more closely for exhibition. They wash and brush swine very carefully
and sometimes curl their pig's tail around a stick or curler.

Exhibitors employ a number of devices in an attempt to modify small
(and sometimes not-so-small) imperfections in the animals. In Ford
County, a group of former exhibitors described some of these:

> A sheep might have a dip in her back and you'd shear her wool to make it
> straight. Course, if he's a good judge, he could feel her, the back without
> the wool, camouflage is what it is.

> Same thing with a cow. The way they stand makes 'em look different, get
> their feet together, arch their back, touch 'em on their feet or their brisket,
> make their back strong when they're pushing on their back.

These ways to clip and trim and train an animal to look more like the dictates of the livestock judging standards are only surface measures that would not fool a thorough judge. Preparers use them but admit the risk; ultimately one does better to produce a decent animal.

Long- and short-term preparation constitute important components of showing in the other major exhibition sections of the fair. An item of clothing, a piece of artwork or a lampshade, or a collection of artifacts may have been conceived right after the end of last year's fair. A quilt with many stitches or pieces might well occupy a year of someone's leisure time. Intricate woodworking, such as a chest or a fretted and carved basket, takes time for planning and execution. Sometimes needleworkers make a special outfit for Thanksgiving or Christmas, which they then decide to bring to the fair seven or eight months later. Mrs. Kelly, an exhibitor in Ford County, described her yearly activities that culminated in fair exhibition:

> Well, I knit, I take lots of things in the home ec department, like a year or two I made a lot of pillows, different things, or appliquéing like Holly Hobby on, then putting a big ruffle around it and just whatever you happen to think of and you look at the material and think, well, what'll I do with that?

She added that she and her husband have four grandsons of whom they take lots of pictures, as do all of the family members of each other throughout the year. Therefore, they also always enter the photographic division every summer with their year-round family album.

Exhibitors plant flowers, crops, and other plants at the beginning of the growing season with hopes for good weather and favorable conditions. As in the raising of animals, the cultivator retains limited control over the product apart from genetic manipulation. He or she weeds, fertilizes, nourishes, protects, and exhorts, and after that the only other power an exhibitor exercises is that of choice of what and when to pick.

Close to fair time, exhibitors choose their finest produce and complete their handicrafts and cooking to bring to the fair. They pick the most perfect looking (according to their tastes and the tastes of their peers) as near to the fair opening as possible. In some cases, this means several hours before the fair begins. Gardeners furbish up their flowers and vegetables for arrangements and display in much the same manner as exhibitors treat their animals. They wash and buff and shine their vegetables. If trimming is called for in the premium books, they carefully barber the leeks and carrots. Exhibitors choose flowers for shape and color. They then arrange them in jars or beakers or in formal permutations. Sometimes they try to finish their actual preparation at the fair so as not to damage delicate materials, but superintendents discourage this because of the chaos generated when all the exhibitors frantically arrange their entries while the fair is being set up. Field crops are sifted (if in grain form), washed (if ears of corn) and examined for bugs, dirt, weeds, and other intruders. Exhibitors coax grain stalks into sheaves. One exhibitor I talked with "knew just exactly how to fix that: tie it up in a little bunch and the top would be so pretty and droop over."

Exhibitors prepare canned goods almost a year before the fair because canning takes place in the fall, after the fairs have been held, and that summer's crop has been harvested. The canner puts aside his or her exhibition jars so the contents won't be mistakenly consumed before they can be shown. Other culinary items should be baked or selected (as in the case of eggs) as close to fair time as possible. Cooks stay up all night preparing food to show at the fair. Jane Turner entered most of the baking categories one year and was intensely occupied with chocolate chip cookies, pound cake, and brownies for the whole weekend before the fair. Freezing allows the organization of some things further in advance, but bakers believe it changes the quality of the goods so do not often choose the option. It may also be that they prefer not to lose the excitement and sensory appeal of last-minute preparation. The last minute is also when the dexterous complete craft projects and needlework in order to have them ready in time for the fair. Exhibitors clean and press and mount these works in frames or on hangers and often just barely finish in time. This feast of intensified encounters with one's life increases the excitement and increases the festival facet of the experience.

The Process of Evaluation at the Fair

The judging and exhibition procedures by which criteria are developed and displayed come from an elaborate and ritualized set of actions and interactions on the part of participants. Exhibition and evaluation of work at a county fair are performances in which the interactions of the participants—judges, exhibitors, and audience—set examples and create changes for future, similar work.

When fair time comes, competitors take their entries to the fair and fill out cards. On these cards they write their names, addresses, and classification or category numbers for their entries and occasionally add a description or recipe. The exhibitors pay a small entry fee, between fifty cents and two dollars. They receive an exhibit number which identifies them and their work during the judging and subsequent placing and when the entries are picked up after the fair. Then, in front of each exhibit, the superintendents put cards that show only the exhibitor's number and the number of the class being judged. Livestock pens carry these cards on the front of their gates. In livestock exhibition, the exhibitors wear the numbers on their backs, thus identifying closely with the animals.

When the time comes for judging, the procedure differs somewhat between livestock and all other categories. In the judging of livestock, the ritual always separates the animals from their private stalls and provides for their public display—in the show ring. The owners or raisers lead out the animals in each class and march them around the ring in a circle. In showing pigs, it is more a matter of simply keeping up with them. Then the exhibitors line up the animals or, if pigs are being shown, confine them in portable pens. The judge walks up and down, stands in the center looking at the animals some more, compares the animals with each other, and feels the bone structure, fat, muscle, hides, and coats. All of this takes place in dramatic silence. Finally the judge slaps one on the rump, signifying first place, after which the audience breaks into applause; another slap on another animal for second place brings more applause, and so on for third and fourth. The superintendent's assistants rush to distribute ribbons and to record the names and placings in the books. The contrast of the slow and silent moves of the judges with the rush of the superintendents gives rhythm and significance to the actual examination of animals as well as to the final pinning on of ribbons. The judge, usually male, goes to the microphone. He announces the placings and gives his reasons, with a commentary on each beast, and in some cases, the deportment of the exhibitor. Sometimes he gives an overview of the whole class of animals on show.

In a few situations, judges test animals for performance (in local terms, efficient weight gain in relation to time and amount of feed consumed) by weighing them in January and again at the county fair in the summer. These figures measure rate of gain and usually apply to market animals rather than breeding stock. This makes sense because the desired end of market animals is the stockyard, as many and as often as possible for the

Figure 4.5   Circling the livestock, Ozaukee County, Wisconsin

pocket of the breeder. Occasionally the procedure will include a little quick learning on the part of the judge. Sam Rogers said,

> The judge one time had never seen one [a Tunis, a form of Blushing Suffolk breed] so the people with the sheep brought him a little booklet during the judging so he would know what the finer points of them were and that way he could judge their sheep more finely.

The judges and performers never distance themselves a great deal from each other. Usually, though, the judges do not refer to external information aids. The mystique of the judge demands a certain knowledge and confidence born of experience.

In all the other categories, if the judging is open to the public, the judges follow two possible procedures. One method allows the items to be brought to a table, category by category, class by class. Often the judge prefers this procedure because the display pattern in the exhibit halls does not always match the premium book order. Also, the welter of other exhibits does not distract the judge. Great concentration characterizes judging time. It is a time of comparison, a time to judge something against its peer. Mrs. Hodge, a Domestic Arts superintendent, gave a sample of the needlework judging:

> I have two girls work ahead of the judges and two behind and they bring out all the stuff to be judged and they lay it all out on a separate table. The whole category is right there on that table for her to see.
>
> And then she picks out first, second, and third, and then I have the other two girls put on the ribbons.
>
> Then I write down in the book what she's done.

In an alternative method, the judge moves from exhibit to exhibit. Sometimes, the judges allow exhibitors to follow them and watch as the judging progresses. This often works best when the exhibits are cumbersome or fragile. It is not a good idea to risk injuring some of the delicate plants by the judges or their assistants needlessly handling them. Sometimes judges find it easier to move from picture to picture on a wall or from wedding cake to wedding cake.

Judging should be conducted with great attention to minute qualities that distinguish one entry from another. The judge will take all the vegetables of a like category—say, green peppers—and examine them all at once in absorbing detail. Thomas Hawley continued the description of judging, this time for vegetables:

> And we'll probably have anywhere from twenty-five to thirty entries, 'cause everybody said, "Oh, I have such nice peppers. I had to bring 'em." Fine. When the judge gets down to turning 'em upside down and counting the points on the bottom, they should have four. Some have five, six, some have three. But he gets right down to counting those points.
>
> And they put their potatoes and their tomatoes in a basket just so.
>
> So you'd think all he did was just look over the top and judge. But he doesn't. We get a table and he takes everything out of the basket and *really* looks it over.

In the Culinary Department the judges cut into the cakes, pies, and breads in order to examine texture, odor, consistency, and taste. Sometimes

Figure 4.6   Judging bread, Ford County, Illinois

the visual attributes do not reach a superior level but the other qualities together make the entry the best in the class. Most judges think savor is most important, but Paula Hornlein explained:

> When you're judging for an audience watching like that, see, first thing they're going to say when they see that *awful*-looking frosting with a blue ribbon on it, they're not going to know what the situation is.

> So you just have to adjust your judging so that you're satisfying both looks and taste.

Occasionally the culinary judge (usually female) offers samples of the baked goods to the audience after she has tested them. Judges open jellies to check texture but not other canned goods, because they will spoil. Usually different judges evaluate different sections of the fair; for example, one judges vegetables and another one judges agricultural produce, or one judges junior needlework and another one open class needlework. If one judge in a similar section finishes and another is behind, however, he or she might assist the other. In some fairs the volume can be staggering, but the degree of difficulty really depends on the proportion of judges to entries. Then, as Mrs. Hodge described, when the judging ends, the ribbons are posted, the results are entered in the book so that winners can pick up their premium money, and the discussion from the audience begins. Jane Turner thought watching the judging was helpful,

> because then if you wondered how come you got the rating you got or if you didn't receive a rating then you'd know the reasons why and you could ask questions right then. . . . that's one of my favorite places to go, is when I take the things and then I'm anxious to see how I come out and then you can talk that over and make suggestions.

Judging facilitates the development of criteria through interaction rather than fiat.

Sometimes the judging is closed, because of time problems or space problems or worries about audience members unconsciously or consciously trying to influence the judge's opinion through indiscreet comments like "Oh, *that* looks nice." In such cases, the judges write comments on the entry cards or discuss their results with the superintendents. Then the conscientious superintendents later attempt to relay these reasons to the exhibitors who ask.

This interplay between judges and exhibitors together with the nature of the judging and exhibition procedure ensures a certain conservatism. Exhibitors mentally reject the decrees of judges who are too extreme in their judgments. They will not complain out loud to the judge, but if enough people voice an objection to the board or refuse to enter the following year, the judge might be rejected from the fair the next year or the year after. Judges may influence style, but not when *their* criteria are judged absurd by the fairgoers. If several judges for several years or in several locations made the same series of judgments, those who take note either might put this down to fad or might begin to look seriously at the provenance of these judgments.

The *performance* of judging and exhibition involves the notion of *en-*

hancement.[2] *Enhancement* includes the special attention to and the heightened awareness of both the act of creating and the act of showing through the judging process. The special intensity arises throughout the compressed time frame; the highlighted reserved places for exhibition; and the costumes and markings or trappings, such as white for dairy exhibitors, and special notebooks and measuring sticks for the horticulture judges—all identifications either outside of or intensifying the normal. The stillness of the hushed voices and loudspeakers, the parade with the slowed-down walk for the animals, and the absorbed silence of judges who examine flower arrangements and the points on the ends of peppers help the judges make a contract with the audience for this special time and situation. This contract says on the part of the judges: you are special, I am paying attention, giving care, and I am *competent* to perform. On the part of the audience and exhibitors it says: we accept your authority, we will listen to your words. In a sense, the exhibitors and audience evaluate the judges through their notice.

Competence as used in performance theory refers to the judges' behavior, the exhibitors' appearance and deportment, and to the materials they have raised or created. *Competence* means the knowledge and ability to perform in socially appropriate ways, to perform both ritual and artifact. The ritual of judging allows the contract to be made and evaluation to take place, for all participants to articulate and accept (as a group, even if not individually) community-based standards. The exhibitors pay a certain amount of attention to these standards and alter their artifacts—swine or quilts—accordingly in varying degrees. Thus the text emerges through social interaction and negotiation.

Perform and show carry the paradox within themselves of surface and depth. *Performance* means the formal or ritualized exhibition of skill or talent. *To perform* also means to execute, accomplish, effect, and fulfill. In other words, *performance* conveys a set of active and by implication participatory processes between audience and performer or between performers. To execute or *fulfill* here refers to the carrying out of a plan, intent, or agreed-upon requirements. The appropriate judging behavior and the criteria for judging are made up of the requirements, or the conceptual plan that orients the participants in their daily lives.

Show concerns the presentation of the surface, of a crafted combination of elements in order to reveal, manifest, make evident by behavior or outward sign. Similar to performance but with a nuance of look rather than act, even in the case of contenders showing animals, show makes a spectacle, or displays for viewing. The spectacle or presentation to view involves

Figure 4.7   Crafts judging, Ford County, Illinois

outward or visible signs or actions intimating something deep, inside. Judging and exhibition not only display the cultural rules (the plan, the requirements) but tacitly agree to execute or complete them—the contract. This fulfillment (in the form of ritual and exhibition of the finished product) of plans, intentions, or agreed-upon requirements signifies an exterior relating to an interior, the representation concretely embodying the abstract. These encompass the concerns of the core of the county fair, which are to involve the community, to perform talent and accomplishment, to perform cultural rules, and to show or make manifest those rules. Through this dynamic interaction of surface and depth, of participants and ritual, the texts (cows, quilts, canned beans)—and through the texts, values—emerge. The sequence becomes look, act, incorporate.

Some of the values emphasize action. Versatility and keeping up with changes, knowing one's field well, and knowing one's colleagues demonstrate mastery in one's vocation. Attention to detail and looking at "minute distinguishing qualities" reveal the precision admired here. Taking the time to examine the exhibits on the judges' part and to prepare the exhibits for show on the part of the entrants indicate the value of care and concentration. Depth is important; what is underneath counts as much as the surface of an animal. Seams on a garment are as important as color combination. These characteristics combined show concern regarding differentiation and distinction among seemingly similar items. This differentiation operates metonymically, substituting the item exhibited for the differentiated exhibitor.

Responding to and articulately addressing the community brings out a further set of values. Those who exhibit understand that nothing exhibited can be perfect. They understand this in part because of their comprehension of the relativism of the judge's decisions. In all departments, judges, superintendents, and exhibitors told me, "No two judges judge alike." A general standard exists that allows individuals to enter and to judge with some consistency. But Ed Luseby said, "There's probably more difference in the individual than from community to community. . . . a good animal in Champaign might be a good animal in Missouri. But not necessarily is the champion bull for a show the best for a given area." Exhibitors and judges remain fairly philosophical about the individual differences that will designate one entry as a first-place winner and another as a second. They admit that sometimes their philosophy fails momentarily at the fair, but in describing the procedures in our interviews during the winter, they calmly explained the nature of personal variation between judges.

One judge may upset another judge's ideas of what a first place might be. An animal could be in first place one day at a show and third place the next with another judge. It will almost never be at the bottom, because evaluators tend to agree on the top range of exhibits. The nuances of change, however, raise a special issue with organic exhibits, including some food products, because all of them can change slightly with time. Flowers or farm produce can droop or wilt or bulge in distressing places, and some livestock have good and bad days. Even when exhibitors prepare or pick food and plants the same day that they are judged, chemical changes occur that preclude any kind of certainty on the part of the exhibitor about their entry. This of course increases the gamble and concomitant excitement.

But in addition to the problem of slight changes in the item that affect the judge's view, different judges' views will vary slightly. Sam Rogers's experiences with sheep judges illustrate the opinions many hold about all judging:

> The judge does what he wants to do and the way he sees it and everybody has a different opinion.

> You don't find a perfect animal and you can fault any of them and it's a matter of what your pet peeve is—it could be bad feet or it could be a bad mouth and the judge has his own opinions of what things are worse than other things and that's the way he places them.

Sometimes the decision relates to structural components of the exhibits and sometimes to the judge's own ineffable combination of preferences. Sam Rogers continued:

> Some just say, I like this one better. They'll go through the motions. They'll get them all lined up and they'll look back and maybe one'll just . . . catch their eye, you know, that they just like the looks of and they'll move them up a couple of places.

> This is why we always try to trim the heads real pretty because sometimes it will make a real difference in the placing.

The kinds of variation that might constitute a livestock judge's personal decision concerning livestock include (among many others) body thickness, the height, upstandingness or squattiness, correctness of feet and legs, mouth, size, color, droop of ear, and soundness.

In other departments experienced observers also divide out areas of personal variation from a general standard. In many cases, they do not disagree about *what* is important so much as differ in their emphasis on varying components or combinations of decision making. For instance, in needlework, Mrs. Denham and Mrs. Kelly (exhibitors of needlework at the county fair) said that the judges would look at color, workmanship, neatness, and overall appearance. Mrs. Denham also said, when asked about the reasons for the judge's final placement of ribbons:

> Whatever appealed to the judge, that's what I always said. If she liked blue, she would pick blue and that was the way it worked with judges.

> It's very different every year. No two judges are going to judge the same, anyway.

Personal preferences for certain kinds of fabrics, materials, forms, and styles of workmanship influence the judge's decision. If a judge loves kittens, the photographs of kittens are going to have an edge in the animal photography section. If the judge dislikes macrame hanging baskets, those will suffer a little in the macrame crafts category. A responsible judge tries to evaluate his or her aversions and prejudices. If judges think their personal predilections obtrude, they sometimes will withdraw themselves just for that category. But most competitors usually accept the notion that one judge approves of extreme sweetness and another abhors it in cakes. Paula Hornlein said, "There again you're going to rely on the judge and what she thinks is a good spice cake. It isn't absolute." The feeling persists that any glaring deviation from an accepted standard is obvious and faulted. But within a standard deviation falls a range of personal idiosyncrasy. Entrants understand this even if they do not always gracefully accept it. As Al Gordon said, "And if it was a real close class, you might have ten judges and ten winners. It's not likely but it's possible."

Along with variations between judges within an accepted standard, judges and exhibitors perceive those same variations between each other. Many times an exhibitor understands perfectly well the nature of the standards and even perhaps the nature of the particular judge who may be officiating for his or her category. Still, the exhibitors often choose to act on their own or their family's preferences, knowing that they might not place in the awards of ribbons. When Mrs. Denham was asked if she made things according to what the judge would like, she replied: "No, I just made 'em to suit myself. And I just took 'em to be taking something." The fairgoers, looking at the exhibits after the judging is done, also do not always agree with the judge. Again, usually exhibitors can trace a disagreement to personal likes and dislikes, an emphasis by one person on small, even stitches and an emphasis by another on flat, open-pressed seams. A judge's choice seldom strikes a fairgoer as absolutely outlandish. Mrs. Kelly described the situation well:

> But no one gets really that upset about it. It was sort of a folksy thing and still is, I think. The whole fair, really, and the exhibits, too.

> Well, I think the people who pass by and look at them, just look, and if it's pleasing, they like it. Not everyone would ever agree with the judge. They'd say, "Why did that one get first?"

Jane Turner described several situations in which competitors took things to the fair, especially in Culinary, that they could tell were not going to be appropriate according to the general standard. She said people might have entered things like underdone brownies because that was how their family liked brownies. In most cases this is done knowingly, possibly defiantly, hoping perhaps to change the standards or to be vindicated in their personal or family's judgment if they should happen to win. Or perhaps they hoped to pick up some premium money if there were few or no others in the category. And of course many fairgoers, like Mrs. Denham, enjoy bringing something just to participate, win or not.

The issue of variation corresponds with an element of the definition of folklore, which contends that any true folklore form must vary according to time period, region, group origin, or circumstances under which it is created or used. This variation signals cultural health, that the quilt, song, story, or plowing pattern reflects meaning of particular peoples; the quilt varies from region to region because it expresses ideals, beliefs, and values of different groups. The variation from standards signals vitality, not stamped adherence to a no-longer-useful mode of action.

Creators of county fair entries almost always remain true to their individual conception of a category, although they conform to a general standard. When they do this and are disappointed in the competition results, they sometimes ascribe the results to the judge's lack of knowledge or understanding if it does not seem to be their own competence at stake. One woman said:

I have a girlfriend that took yeast breads this year and she was very disappointed.

She says she was disappointed because her family *likes* it this particular way and maybe she added things to her yeast bread like wheat germ that give it flavor and different texture and the judge maybe wasn't familiar with that and didn't think it was up to the standard.

This community or general standard encompasses a real set of criteria, which most know tacitly and which some people articulate explicitly. It forms the counterpoint to the individual variation. The criteria used to judge the entries, from livestock to bread, are consistent in each class. There are characteristics peculiar to each category, but the general nature of

Figure 4.8   "A real good one,"
Champaign County, Illinois

the judgments stays similar. Ed Luseby said of livestock judging (and this holds true for other departments):

> You could have three steer shows at the county fair with some of the same animals in the same class and one judge might not pick what the other judge did but as a general rule, most judges are pretty close together.

> They are pretty consistent at finding the real good ones.

Individual, familial, or broadly regional differences influence the judging, but the basic standard remains constant. Although it is primarily judges who publicly verbalize these criteria at the fair, exhibitors, viewers, and officials of the fair know the criteria beforehand.

Rebecca Jones said that people find the median of judging, where people agree, through experience:

Well, there's just standards. Your idea of what was really good might be different than mine. But after you consider everything, the same thing would probably come out on top. One or two will be awfully close out of thirty-five or forty.

People often try to exhibit in a class with a few in it in order to win with less competition. They wouldn't respect the batch as much if there weren't other entries, but it might be that the only one there was deserved a blue ribbon.

If you know anything about baking, good is measured against the standard in the observer's mind if they are experienced. You couldn't tell if you'd never done it.

Most participants agree that experience rather than book learning serves as the basis for many of the standards. They tacitly acknowledge that they share this experience. Exhibitors in the region hold common assumptions that enable them to make and accept judgments without too much deviation.[3] The notion of a standard is one that is necessary to those who exhibit, not only in the county fair but in their everyday lives. Common experience permits neighbors to judge each other and themselves. The county fair provides the place to evaluate and articulate, as Jane Turner indicated:

The gal that judged this year *is* a home ec teacher and a lot of things she said, for instance the peanut butter cookies should be a certain way and she rattled off three or four things, when she said 'em, it sounded like sure, that's right, that's what it should be from *my* own background training.

This shared experience helps form what might be called an average of taste. A consensus of individual tastes and a consensus of idea templates leavened with everyday reality and use compose these criteria.[4]

Competitors agree that they must examine categories of criteria and they agree that a certain level of the criteria exists beyond which something is unacceptable. In two different counties, the judging procedures revealed certain standards for wheat bread. Rebecca Jones, in De Kalb County, said that the judge cuts the bread to see if it is tender or tough: "So you see, there's a standard right there. It's either good or it isn't. After you cut it, here it is, how about the color? Was it browned as it should be? If it's burned, anybody could see that." Jane Turner's assessment in Ford County concurs in essentials with that of Rebecca Jones. She said: "Some things should be *done*, there're some things that are okay if they're not quite done. Like if you get things overdone, for instance, breads, and they're dry, well, as a whole, people don't like to eat dry bread, they'd just as soon they were more moist." These examples indicate that exhibitors' conceptions of criteria confidently include "people" and "anybody" in support of their explanations. This confidence is borne out in the essentially smooth operation of the judging and exhibition sections.

Judging and exhibition reveal the importance of the fitting thing in the fitting place and time. By "placing" first, second, or third, exhibitors take one's place in their community, sometimes literally standing up with one's fellows (no one sits down to exhibit livestock) in the livestock judging, and thus acceptance by and of the community. When Jane Turner talks of her appraisal of the judge's criteria for peanut butter cookies in terms of her own background and training, in a sense she is saying, "I belong." Judging and exhibition entail response to the community through public activity. The community member locates herself or himself in this structure of public ritual, and through this structure, in a physical and cultural neighborhood.

Thus, judging achieves importance through the process of uncovering standards, allowing entrants to depart from or adhere to these standards, and in so doing, understand where they fit in their community each year. "Throughout this discussion of conduct, control, criticism, and community, one issue stands out as prominent: the status of norms. There can be no self-control of conduct or self-criticism unless there are norms by which we distinguish the true from the false, the right from the wrong, the correct from the incorrect," writes Richard Bernstein.[5] Of course, this system is entirely relative; each standard or set of norms must be regarded in its particular context; the norms can and do change, and this is part of what the county fair is all about—tracking the changing norms. For the exhibitors, this process, both the interaction with the judges and seeing themselves figuratively next to their peers, reveals them to themselves as individuals as well as community members. Paradoxically, they need the community to understand themselves as separate entities, and they need the public arena to reveal their private desires. Whether or not they agree with the standards, the standards provide a structure, and through that structure, a sense of identity and belonging. Of course, sometimes this location of self in community comes as an unpleasant revelation.

The judging can reveal lack of belonging to the community. In the same way that individuals change their opinions over the years as the result of many different circumstances, the standard shifts through time as well. This can cause consternation, especially among those whose standards have remained constant. Those who change often enjoy keeping up with the times or they accept social and economic pressures. But some find it exceptionally hard to learn one standard and then have to adjust to a new one, regardless of personal preference.

In livestock this presents a particular problem because changes take much time and money to effect. Mr. Beckman, a livestock superintendent, told me of a man who had raised the most beautiful consistently prize-winning Angus cows. This breeder could not find it in him to change from an older standard. "This fellow was very unhappy, thought the breed had gone downhill, but the truth is, everything changes. That's difficult with a guy that's been so successful."

Techniques and visions that do not change as regards the raising of livestock will presuppose a lack of prizes at the fair, lack of recognition, and subsequently a lack of buyers. Failing to keep up with the standards will shift one from the mainstream or the average without the exhibitor's volition. In order to remain the same in status and recognition, you must change.

This interaction of idiosyncratic taste and criteria and standard taste and criteria is complex. It resembles a fugue in which the strands come together and separate in an underlying pattern but with unexpected variation. The interaction depends heavily on a trait that some in the county fair characterize as typicality or essence, and it always accompanies the concept of proportion. Paula Hornlein summed up the interaction of individual and standard here:

> I have done a lot of judging in 4-H fairs and there is going to be a certain amount of personal preference in there no matter what you do. Just like anything you judge.
>
> If you judge a hog, no three judges will judge it the same. They all have things *they* like to look for in that particular breed.
>
> And it's the same way in baking or cooking. You're going to have a certain amount of your own preference or taste that's going to get in there.
>
> But there are also some standard things that have to apply to it, too. If you're going to be judging a chocolate cake, if you're in a devil's food class, for instance, okay, you want that to have the character that a devil's

food cake should have. Not a milk chocolate cake or a bitter chocolate cake or something like that. You're looking for a more or less definite taste and a definite texture.

We had one year where the woman had put a lot of food coloring into her cake and her cake came out almost as red as your sweater, maybe not quite. It might have tasted fine but aesthetically it was not quite right.

[It should have been brown?]

Yes. You're looking for whatever is typical of that particular thing. But it's kind of hard sometimes to pull both sight and taste together so that you come out with something that's going to be a blue-ribbon product.

The notion of the ideal joins the personal/standard fugue. Nearly all judges and exhibitors carry a template of an ideal. This ideal configuration of whatever it is that they're making or judging is not the same as the standard. Whereas the standard consists of the basic minimum criteria that most share in order to have a common basis for appreciation, the ideal reveals a collection of characteristics forming a perfection that they can never reach. The standard indicates a more impersonal, more group-oriented concept that individuals make, but it tends to exist in relatively changeless form. The ideal may vary more widely from individual to individual. The ideal is really a product of, but separate from, the synthesis of the standard and the individual. It forms a good example of the dialectical process because the ideal then returns in its own form to engage with the standard and individual once again. Ed Luseby's description of the ideal shows how it forms:

> A good judge, once they've learned to look for certain things, you develop an ideal picture.
>
> In my room I have hanging on my wall a picture of an ideal Brown Swiss cow.
>
> On my wall I have a picture of what I call an ideal perfect bull, some bull that my family had.
>
> I thought they were excellent. I still think they're excellent, you know.
>
> And, on my wall, I have a picture of some sheep that I thought were ideal conformation.

You develop and have a feel for it and once you find one that is good and has good production records, then you mentally take a picture of it and you just simply say to yourself, I know this is sound form, this is good form, this is the profitable kind.

So that when I go out and look at animals, after seeing thousands, I mentally have an idea. . . . I'm comparing it to the one I have in my mind as an ideal.

An ideal creates a conception of something existing in its most excellent or perfect form—a perfect model illustrating an idea or vision.[6] Every judge holds this vision in his or her mind against which to compare the item at hand. Every breeder or maker formulates a concept in his or her mind that gives a goal to work toward in creation. The exhibitor or judge learns his or her ideal from extensive experience with his or her own area of expertise and interest, his or her own personal experiences, and from an understanding of the consensus that makes up the standard. Paula Hornlein points out:

This of course is where your judge has to be a qualified person, a home ec person who really knows her fluids, knows what she's looking for, knows what the taste is.

The judge we have in particular is excellent. When you go through your cookies or your quickbreads in particular, we have a lot of nuts and she can tell you right off the bat what's not so fresh or otherwise been sitting around a lot. And if it's got too much cocoa in it or too much of this, she knows.

But the variation that exists in everyone's own experience with his or her own field injects the personal component into the formation of the ideal. Therefore, each judge and exhibitor holds a marginally different ideal. Given the nature of judging at the county fairs, however, these ideals are forced into tolerant coexistence with each other. The judging system at the fairs molds itself on the realistic workings of its world.

This model shows the individual, the community, and the concept of the ideal in the evaluation process. In actuality, the concept of the community becomes paramount. The judging process imposes a reconciliation of the ideal with the normative and this is understood by the judge and the exhibitor. The process makes room for individual judgment but establishes in time the community as the ultimate arbiter.

Rather than judging against an unobtainable ideal, evaluators generally judge exhibitors against each other. Community members understand that the ideal, or perfection, never can be reached in life, especially since the ideal varies so idiosyncratically. They carry the ideal in their head, but they exhibit and are judged according to what exists at the fair at that moment. And they realize that with a different set of judges or exhibitors the results could be different the next day or the next hour.

Each item entered in a class gets judged against the others entered in its class. The judge *must* award a blue ribbon in Illinois. If it is the only item in a class, the judge will sometimes write or discuss why it does not live up to the standard or ideal, just to be sure that no one is "getting away with something." As Rebecca Jones pointed out earlier, however, it still could be a very good quality item, and people will then judge it in their minds from their experience of other items, just as if there were other entries. The participants acknowledge an ideal, just as they acknowledge personal idiosyncrasy, but they also agree that it (the ideal) might never be reached because of the singular preferences of judges and exhibitors, or because the ideal does not exist in the pool available for judging. The community is judged against itself. A group of officials at Sandwich Fair discussed this:

> [Frank Weaver:] You can only have one first and that's where the judge comes in. There's only one blue. . . . If there's only two entries, the judge has to give first and second. One entry *must* be awarded a first premium. . . . he [the judge] may say, I wouldn't even have that on my—
>
> [Interjection by Sam Warren:] It's the best that's being *shown.*
>
> [So it's always the best in a class, not the best absolutely?]
>
> That's right.
>
> [Frank Weaver:] And it irritates people who see inferior stuff that they wouldn't think would be entitled to a first premium but our regulations say you must award firsts. On the theory, as Sam says, that it was the best of that which was displayed.

Through this process participants reinforce the localness of the judging. The winner produces the quintessential one of its kind at the time of the judging. The ideal lives in the minds of particular participants, but it shifts because of local community circumstance. The idea of the community within the ideal predominates, not an absolute, discouraging, unobtainable ideal. The community can be the pool of items to be judged or the people who hold common interests. The ideal is acknowledged as an individual goal or guide, but the presence or absence of peers constitutes the real basis of decision. And implicitly, peers want everyone to do their best. If someone gets a blue ribbon for a poor product, it seems as though that was the best the community could offer. And no one feels happy with that idea. Sometimes that issue even spurs fairgoers on to enter, in order to show what a *really* good entry can be and thus elevate the implied standard of the community.

Since judges judge normatively, looking at what is present rather than what is absent, judges dislike the situation described earlier in which they must evaluate across categories. It is much more difficult to reconcile ideas of normative and ideal in judging dissimilar items. There exists less basis for formal comparison. A more abstract standard comes into effect of necessity. Sam Rogers told of one kind of situation and the resolution:

> In junior show you get champion over all breeds.

> No judge likes that class—you can't really judge one breed against another. What he does is pick the one that most represents the breed. . . . the judge would have in mind what he would like in all the breeds, and the one that most fits what he has in mind, he'd put in that one.

> And he aims, too, for the most perfect sheep over all breed (trying to leave out specific breed characteristics) mouth-wise, leg-wise, body-wise.

The normative background to this kind of judging dominates because the judge still looks for the best sheep representative of each breed in its way. Then they judge these against each other for ideal sheepness.[7] The same holds true of something like crafts, where the difficulty escalates in judging metalwork properties with needlework. Abstract qualities like amount of effort displayed, neatness, good taste, and propriety of execution become criteria to be judged against each other after each has been judged in reference to its own class or normative standard. Now judges evaluate these entries according to the larger community normative standards. They look for the best done in each class and then compare those to a normative standard of workmanship when judging across classes. This kind of class seems to highlight the more usual, community normative procedures by departing somewhat from that procedure, much the same way that "odd" categories highlight serious ones and that the carnival frames and reinforces the judging and exhibition activities. Because it is an aberrational form, somewhat incorporating a shift in focus, this judging across categories emphasizes normative judging as the desirable format. It seems to emphasize what most (not all) judges and exhibitors seem to feel are the proper relationships between idiosyncratic opinions, average standards, and an ideal vision.

These relationships form the background to the explicit sets of judgments that comprise the criteria for judging and exhibiting. This description indicates the participants' understanding of a situation that provides a context for the criteria and shows how they deal with the anomalies, the lack of perfection, and the differences in opinion that eventually result in the promulgation of tacit and explicit criteria. In these cases, although the individuals who compose the criteria make up the community, the criteria take on an existence separate from community. The criteria influence the same community of individuals that made them. These criteria are established through the concepts of the ideal, the community, and the individual, and may be altered by a combination of these factors.[8] Any one of these alone will seldom possess the power of these combinations to influence the criteria. Optimistically, people reach a consensus rather than trying for something that can never exist—they judge for a reality rather than for a heartbreaking ideal that is idiosyncratic, perfect, variable, and meaningful only to the individual.

Chapter Five

"Eye Appeal"/Aesthetic Criteria for Judging

Ed Luseby, livestock judge, Animal Science professor at the University of Illinois, and one person who characterized himself as having a direct relation with art, said (apropos of developing a system of judging standards), "Art is looking at them. Science is the efficiency of performance (rate of gain in an animal). Put them both together and you have Progress." Ed Luseby told me that his friend L. E. Mathers of Mason City, Illinois, and the best cattleman that Ed had ever met, elaborated on this when talking about judging:

> The one that has the ability to judge livestock is just like a good artist. You know, a good artist knows the form and the lines and the things that all blend together to make it a beautiful painting.

> A good livestockman knows the lines, knows the form, and should know what makes an animal best suited for a particular purpose. Long and tall and heavy-muscled and correct-legged and all of these things go together.

> But again, this is where judgment comes in—judgment to see which is the
> best one. This is art.

People choose to enter their creations at the county fair because they have
made something and they want to show it off. They enter because they became inspired by the fair book or last year's fair, which impelled them to
try new ideas or techniques or to outdo their neighbor. Exhibitors show to
satisfy the competitive instinct, to get criticism, to learn, and to see how
they measure against their peers. They want to see how they fit into the critical system and they want to help influence it.

> You can go to the fair and compare your best livestock you got with the
> best of somebody else's. If you don't take that as constructive criticism . . .
> but it can be educational, the state statute says it's an educational exhibit.

> It's probably the best whether in livestock or cakes, you're proven the one
> who knows how to do it. . . .

> Some place you need to compare the best you have with some of the better
> hogs and see how you stack up.

Judging and exhibition orient the participants to their own professional and
moral environment. This statement of William Beckman, swine breeder
and county fair swine superintendent, locates some of the criteria. Seeing
"how you stack up" permits the exhibitor to set him or herself right by ad-
justing (or not) to the principles of peers and the market. Comparing "the
best you have with some of the better" educates participants as to their
bearings in their social and economic community by dramatizing the criteria, the elements characterizing the values of the group. These criteria represent the touchstone, the authenticity of intangible beliefs about how to
create and live an agricultural life.

Judging and exhibiting of specimen blooms or homemade Christmas
ornaments or table settings for Sunday dinner publicize the criteria. The
criteria develop continually. The realm in which participants determine and
describe these gauges of achievement replicates itself throughout county
fairs. The framework of that realm allows for variation within a defined
structure, somewhat in the manner of a sonnet. Like the physical sections
of the county fair, the cores seem stable with provision for change at the
edges. Over time, the ideal for animal type changes. Bakers use less sugar
for peach pies. To a large extent, the criteria evolve in relation to commu-

nity opinion, time of showing, range of items displayed, nature of the judge, nature of each exhibitor, and nature of the particular fair. The most competent people in the community pride themselves on composing an entry that responds to all of these elements. Through these compositions participants create a product, whether it be sheep or a 4-H project on citizenship, that represents thought and dexterity and arrangement (of self and product) in proper orderly form.

Getting the Standard: The Judges' Acquisition of Rules for Measure

Members of the community influence the formation of characteristic elements in the same way they do the formation of categories and the execution of judging. For one thing, the judges learn their standards and form their ideals through a variety of sources. Dr. J. M. Dodd described the process:

> The community influences me some through reading, going to shows and seeing animals placed, complaints and comments afterwards, especially when you're starting out. . . .

> Some breeder who had the reputation for being a real good judge, he'd come around and he'd say, "Dodd, you missed that one. . . . look at the difference in the top line. . . . see how when you walk behind her, she walks with her hocks in and her feet out." . . .

> Anytime you get so old you can't learn, you're done.

Judges learn through university and breeders' organization courses, through other people's ideas, the consumers at the store, journals, Agricultural Extension Service bulletins, and experience. The judges learn their criteria as a distillation of the criteria of those they are judging. Other people's ideas contribute some of the components by which judges evaluate exhibits. Sometimes the concepts arrive through the kind of direct comment at the fair that Dr. Dodd's recitation described. Exhibitors often come and talk to the judges and officials after the judging ends. When I asked Jane Turner if she would give her ideas to the judge, she replied,

> Usually you just listen to what the judge has to say, you kind of feel the temperament of the judge, some are more welcome to suggestions than others, but sometimes you would say, is this an acceptable method and I would explain how I did it. . . .

I'm thinking now especially with clothing, that they hadn't seen it done
that way, they might think, well, that works in that situation, that will be
fine.

Sometimes these opinions influence the judge, who may alter an idea for
the next judging. Comments during the judging are strictly forbidden but
conversations afterward have become part of the judging process.

Those who exhibit and actively work in their field influence the
judge's understanding of standards outside the county fair as well as in. Ed
Luseby said:

Oh, I like to visit with the people that exhibit the animals, and things like
that, as a person that's interested in livestock.

Yeah, I learn some from the breeders and exhibitors because some of them
are astute people and intelligent people. . . .

And you know, I like to sit down with the man that raises them, and talk
about them. Go out in his pasture or go out in his feed lot, wherever they
might be and look at them and talk with the people, you know, that you
think are intelligent, honest, and progressive, this is where you get it, you
know.

Community members also indirectly influence a judge's choice through
hiring and firing. The judges who follow the outlines of the decisions about
value that the exhibitors as a group find acceptable are the judges whom the
county fair officials retain. The exhibitors carry a good deal of weight in regard to which judges are hired and fired. Mrs. Fawcett and Mrs. Wilson of
the arts and crafts section at the Sandwich Fair feel that community members change the judges' propensities through insisting that the judges of
whom they approve or disapprove be hired or fired, so that they accept or
reject the judges' tastes.

The Hawleys discussed how the vegetable and horticulture judges establish their gauges of excellence. They mentioned that these judges get
their training from school or classes during the winter from state agriculture departments. However, mere courses alone will not qualify a judge in
their eyes, nor will mere experience. Courses help judges to learn the
state's rules and regulations. But then they need to apply the rules to real-
life situations, just as store and orchard owners must learn to put these rules
in practice so that their customers will buy their products. Economics, dic-

tated in part by the consumers, lowered the demand for lard (because of easy spoilage and because of dietary changes for health reasons) and thus has changed the yardsticks for a good hog. Formerly, a good hog was a fat hog; this is no longer the case. Judges now look for lean hogs. David Spivak explained that judges average out their criteria between the university's specifications, their own ideas, other people's ideas, and reports from consumers via the stockyards and the breeder's checklist:

> And because of the livestock buyer at the stockyards, they want this type because this is what the consumer's gonna want, this is what the buyer's gonna want. Eventually this is what the breeder has to raise and this is what the judge is eventually going to be looking for.

These symbiotic relationships indicate that no *one* source may take sole responsibility for dictating the touchstones for a really good cow or baby bonnet. Producers and arbiters influence each other by this process and know they have the power to do so. If the government says canning should be for three hours, it says so in part because it has consulted with home economists who can food and know the safe time for old-fashioned canning. If it doesn't work, producers and breeders ignore the rules or change them. County fair participants create a small environment where they can control their economic world through their aesthetic culture.

Remember that almost all these people occupy, or have occupied, more than one role, either simultaneously or at different times. They might show in one fair, judge at another, and act as an official or superintendent at yet another fair. Often they attend fairs with which they claim no official connection, just for the connoisseur's pleasure. They almost all judge from more than one viewpoint. Many judges judge on the basis of experience as exhibitors, breeders, home economists, craft store or florist shop managers, newspaper photographers, and seed corn salespersons. Not only are they aware of community standards, they *are* the community.

Getting the Standard: The Exhibitors' Acquisition of Rules for Measure

Since these people play different roles at different times of their lives, it follows that exhibitors would derive their sense of criteria from much the same sources as the judges. This makes for a theoretically happy consonance between judges and judged. However, not all judges have been exhibitors and not everyone has access to the same sources of information and training, such as breeders' seminars, market surveys, fashion shows, or seed journals. Generally, while most judges emphasize special classes to teach them to be masters of their subjects, and diverse experience gained in the professional pursuit of their interests, exhibitors emphasize professional organizations, classes to teach them the basics of their subjects, and personal experience gained through social or professional activities.

For instance, breeder's associations play a large part in determining livestock standards for exhibitors. Ed Luseby outlined the workings:

> Well, they have groups of people that get together. . . .
>
> Part of the standards of judging, say, Polled Whitefaced Hereford cattle, they're probably set by members of an association, breeders themselves that get together periodically and say, "This is the standard that I'd like to see."
>
> In other words, they'll take a photo and say, "This is the form we'd like to see."
>
> Now today, they sit down and say, "This is the growth rate that we'd like to see and this is the performance we'd like to see," and they're set by breeders and breeders' associations.

These experienced breeders have raised livestock and produced animals and have read the books as well. The breeders' associations produce a synthesis of the available information appropriate to that time. The Rogerses try to go to their Illinois Lamb and Wool Association's Shepherd's Holiday and Symposium because of the chance both to teach and learn about their field. Louisa Rogers said, "They have programs you can go to, people from out of state, university breeders, plain old sheepmen. They give talks on what they're doing with housing, breeding, rearing lambs." Through these activities interested parties absorb new techniques, exchange information, and establish a consensus by which to raise and implicitly to judge their animals.

At these livestock association meetings specialists come and give classes or lectures in particular subjects. Louisa Rogers described a woman from a woolen mill in Iowa who discussed the handling of woolen fabrics with her audience, who contributed some of their notions, too. These special classes follow the Home Extension model.

Home Extension has exerted influence on this region since the 1930s. Women from every county attend classes and sometimes help teach them. These classes teach new skills that establish the "right" and the "wrong" way of doing things. Teachers impart the standards along with the techniques. Knitting should be so tight or so loose; vegetables should look this bright or this faded when being canned; sugar flowers should be within a certain range of colors for cake decorating. The extension service, as part of the state government, operates with the considerable aid of the state university. People attend regular classes in their neighborhoods and special events at the University of Illinois. The extension service acts as the university extended into the home and it operates on the cell system. A few learn and then go teach others, who then teach more in an ever-multiplying organism.[1] Mrs. Kelly (county fair exhibitor of domestic products) said:

> The University of Illinois extension has contributed *a lot* to the education of rural women who hadn't been able to receive any of that training in school. It was good for them . . . to take lessons and present it to the other women. And *that's* how you learn, in doing it yourself.

At one time, extension provided exact methods and standards for turning out products. Mrs. Kelly said, "We really did do things the way they said. There were specific patterns for things then. Now there's a lot of do-it-yourself and change it." Specific lessons for cooking and sewing and doing laundry and papering the walls taught the homemaker new skills. Mrs. Denham, Mrs. Kelly's daughter, said, "We went there to a carpet demonstration and they had all different kinds of carpet and he'd show us what was real good." Now the classes are more generalized and theoretical in terms of content (interior decoration instead of painting and papering the walls) and the methods of learning less rigid. The present generation now in their thirties and forties feel freer to experiment and change. This means they look to Agricultural Extension agents and publications for guidelines in their development of standards but feel more explicitly that they, too, are the authors of the criteria through their own changes and contributions. Since they teach as well as learn, since they adapt as well as implement, students who attend extension classes mold the criteria through community agreement and diverge where they feel it necessary.

Classes of other kinds inspire exhibitors. Mrs. Hodge, county fair domestic arts superintendent, said that the craft stores in particular wield influence because they teach arts and crafts. She explained that the combination of goods carried at the stores gave people an ideal of techniques and standards. Mrs. Denham and Mrs. Kelly confirmed this in another county. They told me that a woman who runs a craft store in Ford County and gives demonstrations at the county fair teaches quilting classes from her store. Mrs. Kelly went to look.

> I just wanted to see how different it would be and those are all handmade [quilts], no pressing.

> She doesn't believe in pressing with an iron, like pressing your seams straight because it stretches it and because she says, "you like that nice puffy look."

So stores and classes disseminate ideas, and like Home Extension, it is an exchange rather than a total imposition.

Many people cited personal experience gained through social or professional activity as a source for the acquisition of criteria. Informal classes held by friends and neighbors spring up for the purpose of teaching knitting, canning, or cake decorating to each other.

Watching parents—"looking over the quilt frame," as Mrs. Kelly put it—taught standards as well. Working alongside family and friends, children learned to cook and to clean and to sew and to plant and to raise animals, and they learned a canon of right ways and wrong ways to do these things. "And you'd be surprised," said Mrs. Denham, "how much you learn, working with others. Walking along the street, there are not two houses that probably cook alike. . . . we learned from the neighborhood. We have a lot of clubs. Everyone belongs to the same things, really."

Criteria into Creation

When people prepare their exhibits for show, they carry these standards in the back of their minds. For some, the standards prevail more than for others. In livestock showing, exhibitors pay higher entry fees and win higher premiums in part because the commercial relationship is more direct than with many of the domestic, plant, or craft exhibits. Therefore, those showing in livestock evince more concern as to preparation in order to meet the judges' standards. Exhibitors in other departments appear to be marginally less involved in worrying about the judge's specific opinion, although they do follow basic criteria in preparing their exhibits. Even if they do not strictly follow those criteria, they certainly know their components.

Livestock preparation can be a long and detailed process in which exhibitors lavish anxious care on the appearance of each animal. They also attempt to adjust (temporarily) structural defects for the show. When exhibitors make these cosmetic changes, they execute them with a precise sense of a series of characteristics that judges and exhibitors, as a rule, will find acceptable.

In Ford County, a group of livestockmen discussed exhibiting techniques that were related to the county fair showing and sets of rules for final products. John Bergner: "Now they take the clipper and take the hair off [the cow], it shows their quarters and makes them look bigger." Al Gordon: "They want the hide to look heavier and rougher, make it [the steer] look heavier." A dairyman in Champaign County elaborated:

> If the animal has like a crooked leg or something, if you sand down or file down one side of her hoof, it'll make her walk more on the other side, it'll make her walk straighter.

> And when you clip, you clip all the hair off the heads and trim the tails and blend in the shoulders and everything, like if she's got kind of a round shoulder then you can cut it short around the sides and tapered towards a point—make it look like she's not so beefy.

A beef showman in Champaign County explained that certain techniques of presentation "might show a leaner appearance to the judge." Another man said they breed and prepare hogs with an eye toward current criteria, as they do sheep. Since leanness is desirable for all animals these days, competitors no longer block (wash and shape with the hands like a sweater) sheep's wool to make the animal look thicker; and they wash and brush and exercise swine so they will look lean and rangy. Beef cattle used to have their tails ratted (teased) to make the animals look blockier. Now, according to John Fennelly, exhibitors fluff the tails at the top and tie and knot at the bottom so that they look tapered.

In the other exhibition departments of the fair, procedure varies from the extreme of "I don't think we ever planned ahead what we were going to take like some people do. . . . why don't we take the pillow, or something that you made," to types who study the winners from last year, read the

Figure 5.1   Fluffing the tails, Henderson County, Illinois

books and craft magazines, and worry about whether the judge will approve. Most exhibitors, of course, fall somewhere in between indifference and anxiety as far as preparation goes.

Knowledgeable entrants stressed that even without conscious effort at the time of making or raising an exhibit, an exhibit's qualities seldom range far beyond or fall far below the basic standards that the community accepts. Very little strays too far out of line. In fact, a judge retains the discretion to reject from the outset an animal, a piece of produce, or a piece of needlework he or she considers unworthy of even being judged. So most experienced exhibitors know and comply with a minimum set of standards if they want their work even to be considered, much less placed.

Jane Turner's opinions and practices typify those of many exhibitors. She feels that she would seldom make anything especially with a judge's eye in mind at county fair time: "That's probably how I'd make the garment anyway and then come fair time. . . . I really didn't have that in mind when sewing it." She says she usually just makes things that she really wants to do to please herself and does not worry about what the judges will like. However, when fair time comes, she makes a choice as to what is good enough to take for public exhibition and competition. This entails some sorting among standards:

> That I didn't do it hurriedly, I had time to finish the seams and press it straight and maybe if I had to make alterations, if I had to take something in, I didn't just take a huge tuck, I took the time and did it right. Well, rather than taking a huge tuck in it, rip it out, take the seam the way it's supposed to, trim off the excess.

"Good enough" clearly implies that she has a list of attributes that distinguish a piece good enough to show from an ordinary item. Most people will take extra care with items for public scrutiny here, but they will not completely subordinate their personal desires to those of the judge. In most cases anyway, the judge's criteria and the exhibitor's criteria resemble each other closely. But the exhibitors feel it is most important that their primary goal be to produce something that satisfies them or their families; something that pleases their sense of criteria in conjunction with basic standards of achievement. At that point they will choose the best from that group or will enter something they have prepared for the fair that specifically meets those conditions.

Entering for competition seems to heighten the care and anxiety with which exhibitors prepare their entries. Exhibitors take special care because of the public circumstances that attend fair competition. People have described that intense period of finishing, cleaning, and arranging immediately before the fair as something a little special, a little different from everyday concerns with cleanliness and propriety. Most folks do not have time ordinarily for the kind of intense preparation that the exhibition necessitates; yet this kind of preparation at least guides operations in daily life. They prove that they are familiar with the rules, the ideal, and the approved mode of doing things by following them for the annual fair when they cannot follow them every day.

These criteria provide a framework within which participants live their daily lives. When Jane Turner bakes a plate of cookies for her family, she does not throw them out if some are small and some are large, if some are dark brown and some are light brown. But she does know that for the fair, and as an ideal to aim for and sometimes reach at home, cookies should be as uniform in size as possible so that they all bake evenly and everyone gets a pretty good, maybe excellent, cookie. She has a model toward which to work. Out of the chaos of many different modes of cookie baking, Jane Turner and her friends and associates are free to accept, reject, and invent because of the set of criteria that are clear to them. They have constructed a basis of order on which to work:

> When, I really like to experiment a lot and I would probably go ahead and use, if I found something really neat from my college experience, I would probably try to substitute that into our family standard recipe and then, if it differs from everyone else's, that wouldn't bother me at all. . . .

> Well, I know people both sides, some people are real anxious to try new and different things, and then other people, if the recipe does not call for it, they will not put it in, they have to follow it exactly, and timewise, baking and if it says to let something rest for thirty minutes, they don't, it can't wait half a day, it has to be just thirty minutes.

> And sometimes I think maybe because I've had more experience with some of these things I know it can be thirty minutes or it can be forty-five minutes, it's not going to damage the outcome.

> (So if extension came out with guidelines, would people follow exactly or modify?)

> I think people would do what they wanted to. I mean, read it, and then maybe try it that way the first time. My personal rule of thumb is whenever I try a new recipe, even though I think maybe it could be changed some, like the amount of sugar could be cut down, that kind of thing, I usually follow the recipe the first time and the next time I put in so much, or more.

The Nature of the Aesthetic

Critical vocabulary reveals the nature of the aesthetic used in executing and judging work. Descriptions of standards for livestock, culinary, needlework, arts and crafts, floriculture, and horticulture remain remarkably consistent; they reinforce each other and, at the same time, are reinforced by the other constructs of the fair. Each department reveals in its turn a near unanimity of values and strengths through the criteria.

Livestock judgments between the different species indicate consistent

Figure 5.2   Baked goods of uniform size, Carroll County, Illinois

concepts of desirability. Today's animal should follow the dictates of L. E. Mathers's earlier description. "Long," "tall," "lean," "rangy," "well-muscled," "correct-legged," and "harmonious structure" detail some of the requisite traits of an animal. As Dr. Dodd elaborated, "A real good cow . . . has a symmetry and a balance of parts and nothing really wrong with it. They have eye appeal." He then developed a complete detailed analysis of the points in judging a dairy cow:

> The purpose of a cow is to give a lot of milk over a big period of time, years. Those high producers are those which are relatively tall for their breed, angular, spacing between the ribs, pin bones are prominent, usually chiselled about the head and long . . . slender in the neck. All will have a good-sized udder.

> And yet you don't want it too big because the big, big ones are too big, too fleshy, subject to injury. A good one is of moderate size, you can milk it till there's very little left, the teats are of good size, even placed so the milking machine will go over the top of them and stay, their udders are high and

wide in the rear, snugly attached to the front. So it stays there and it has a good crease through the middle because that is a main support; when a cow walks, her udder moves, flippity flop, from side to side.

Now a good cow, she has strength, that means she is deep and wide in the chest with good heart capacity. She has a well-sprung rib and depth of body so she can hold a lot of feed in order to get a lot of milk.

Need good feet and legs so they can move around, get their feed, not be uncomfortable. Feet that are sore and arthritic, that cow doesn't feel like working. Sore feet reduces a cow's yield almost as much as disease. . . . There's a certain foot structure that's more likely to become sore on concrete, in the lot. Toes spread, pasterns weak, shallow heel so foot tilts.

Too much bend in the legs, the side view sickle out, that makes 'em walk wrong and if the legs are too straight, then they get crampy.

According to Robert Edwards, dairy cattle should be straight-topped and sharp-cornered. They should have pronounced development of the barrel for feed capacity, and a long face and wide muzzle for eating to show that feed is going to milk rather than body fat. As he said, "She's either putting it on her bone or in the pail, one or the other." Cleanliness and femininity are important. Cleanliness of the cow, and especially her "attachments," or udder, relates to the attractiveness and health of the milk. Femininity also refers to the mammary system and to something less definable yet palpable about the cow. It has to do with a nice adjustment of parts, teats not too short or too long, too fat or too thin, too straight or too crooked, and so with all the attributes of the cow. In short, she should be "uniform" in appearance.

Except for the criteria directly related to milk giving and dairy character, judges gauge all other animals by similar measures. When asked how he would judge good-quality pork, David Spivak jokingly replied, "Well, right off the plate." And Louis Olmert, assistant swine superintendent, concurred. But another swine superintendent, Beckman, seriously backed them up:

A good one, you're looking at a hog that as it moves, you can see muscle move, that is long and lean, that isn't real broad across the top, which all that is excessive fat. . . .

Figure 5.3   Good swine, Green County, Wisconsin

What everyone wants in all livestock is basically an animal that grows fastest and makes the leanest . . . the kind of meat a housewife will buy.

But the biggest can be too fat and the leanest can be too little so you go for the kind in the middle of the road.

He also mentioned uniformity. This breeding characteristic will indicate inheritability of desirable or undesirable traits. "You're looking for repeatability rather than just one fluke animal."

Standards for sheep parallel those for other livestock. Sam and Louisa Rogers said that the general criteria can be summed up by "long, smooth, meaty, firm, and trim." They said meat is the purpose of the whole thing, even if they are showing purebred stock. They also discussed breed types; differences between breeds exist, although in less pronounced fashion than formerly. Therefore some breed characteristics assume significance. Placement and shape of ears, wool thickness and position, and variation in typical color and texture still will make a difference occasionally in a close contest. Structurally these animals are quite similar, but details will divide a first from a second.

When Ed Luseby talked about judging beef animals, he used words
like "efficiency," "soundness," "correctness," "fast growing," and
"longevity." He described the importance of judging the conformation
(form, or the skeleton with the muscles and tendons, what makes an animal
work) in order to judge structural harmony and correctness. He explained
that in purebred animals in particular he looks for longevity because of the
expense of raising them and the qualities that make them a good breeding
animal, characteristic of their role:

> You know, the males ought to look like males, females ought to look like
> females.

> We can look at the genitalia and tell whether they're deformed or not de-
> formed, and you know, an experienced person can do that.

> All the people that argue and say physical form doesn't have any virtue in
> looking at it from that standpoint, well they're wrong. . . .

> We've got to look at them physically to see if they're mother cows,
> whether they're going to have the breeding apparatus so they can breed,
> whether the bulls have the right-sized testicles, look like they're fertile
> animals. . . .

> Just two years ago, a young person had saved some bull calves, and the
> way he saved them was he weighed them at weaning time, and he looked
> for those that had good physical structure . . . usually the ones that are tall
> and long-bodied are frequently going to be faster gainers than the short-
> legged ones and short-bodied ones. We can tell this physically, a good one
> from a real poor one. But we can't tell the best from the best. We have to
> measure this, with a scale.

> Well, he'd saved the four he thought were most promising. And we were
> looking at them and he said, what do you think of that calf? and I said,
> "Jim, there's only one thing wrong with him."

> And he said, "what's wrong with him?" And I said, "He has only one
> testicle."

> And he said "no" and I said "yes, he does, oh yes he does."

> And he looked and he said, "I never saw it, I never saw it."

You know, these are important observations. These are really important observations. And you know, you can't measure that with a scale.

While one or two elements might be superior, it is the best combination of all elements that mandate an excellent animal. Visual appraisal of traits takes on primary importance in establishing and evaluating guidelines for breeding. L. E. Mathers summed it up in his talk with Ed Luseby when he concentrated on "things that all blend together" and "something best suited for a particular purpose."

Most of the foregoing criteria for livestock apply equally to products in other departments. Mr. Mathers's ideal of balance, symmetry, and suitability for purpose characterizes foods, needlework, vegetables and fruits, floriculture, and crafts. In baking, uniformity and balance relate to appropriateness and visual harmony. Jane Turner described the ideal cookies she discussed earlier in connection with everyday baking:

> Eye appeal is so they all look the same. Not a plate of big ones and little tiny ones. And therefore they'll bake more evenly, too, if they're all the same.

> In taste, it should be not too strong in one ingredient, like too salty or too much flour or too overpoweringly sweet.

She reiterated the concept of appropriateness to use and added that something should be characteristic of its class: "Nutbreads are sometimes supposed to have a crack down the middle, so you want to make sure they do and if they didn't, then you start all over again." She mentioned that people do not like very intense colors in cake decoration, especially black or deep purple, and they do not like to eat things that are too "goofy," such as a cake replica of a lady's one-piece undergarment that they got one year. However, a Monopoly board cake done in fine line with inoffensive colors was acceptable and admired. Paula Hornlein said,

> You can tell when you listen to peoples' comments as they go by. The colors that blend well, that look nice, are things that people will think of eating.

> But every once in a while you'll get something that comes in that's maybe a little gaudy you know. The comments are, "Well, we wouldn't want to eat that."

Figure 5.4   Frosted cakes with fine detail, De Kalb County, Illinois

Wedding cakes traditionally display light colors, although they are no longer strictly white (paralleling changes in women's bridal dresses). Commentators stress appropriateness to the occasion. Fine lines of frosting design and frosting texture loom large in the decisions; line and texture determine the durability, recognizability, and difficulty of the decorations. They indicate the peak of subtlety of execution in cake decoration.

Desirable baked goods show even consistency, as in other departments. Rebecca Jones used bread as an example:

> Bread—a crust sometimes could be a little bit wrinkly, not nice and smooth and just maybe not a consistent color . . . spotted. Or browner on one side than another . . . when you cut it, the knife ought to go through evenly, without much resistance. . . . are the little holes even?

> Sometimes the top will be light and open but in the bottom that would be more solid. That would count against it, of course.

> And then the flavor. Sometimes it would taste yeasty, sometimes lacking flavor and sometimes just a real nice taste but doesn't taste of any one thing.

Judges consider evenness an indicator of quality in all parts of the product. It ensures that there are no unpleasant surprises or extremes.

Finally, with baked goods, the issue of homemade products surfaced. Paula Hornlein said that people always ask if something is a "scratch cake" if they think it is good. She said they realize the value of a cake made from elements assembled at home and think it is really better. People think that box cakes are all right; most people do not have time to use anything else. But homemade cakes are "given just a hair more desirability."

Canned goods reveal analogous criteria to baked goods and even to livestock. Further, issues such as clarity of liquid in vegetables or of jams and jellies are involved in the judgment of the typicality of a good product. Butters and preserves are not supposed to be too runny or too rubbery. Critics regard faithfulness to color—meaning not too bleached or overcolored—as essential. Judges hold up jars to the light to check for sediment or cloudiness or sugariness and to estimate trueness of color. Rebecca Jones used green beans as an example:

> Does that look like you had just picked the beans, like it came out of the garden? Or has it changed, if it's been processed a little bit too much, that's affected the color. . . .

> If they're cut beans, if they're cut regularly, it's going to look better than if they are a little one and a big one.

She has added freshness and regularity, evenness of arrangement (which includes issues of proximity) to the height of picked perfection, as the kinds of characteristic traits by which to judge a product. Eggs should be of a uniform size and shape and quite clean. Soap should be fine and smooth. Vinegar should be "the right color" and clear.

Needlework criteria also echo those of the other departments. Garments should show a great deal of work. Seams should be straight. Stitches should be small and even. Jane Turner elaborated: "The construction was the big thing, so that your seams were straight and everything looked the way it was supposed to, it was clipped the way it was supposed to, like it lays flat if it was supposed to, the top stitching's even, details that way." Finishing off work and presenting it in clean, composed condition is absolutely required. Mrs. Denham and Mrs. Kelly added to the needlework store of judging elements:

[Mrs. Denham:] How it's made, how it's made.

[Mrs. Kelly:] Oh, neat seams, are the zippers put in properly, are the hems neat underneath, look at it inside and out, a good hem is one that doesn't pucker or the stitches don't show on the outside. Are the seams finished, open, can it be let out, is it large enough around the neck? Everything's finished, not rough, no raw seams, use binding tape so it doesn't ravel.

[Mrs. Denham:] If you didn't do that right it would ravel out. (With quilts or pillows) it's the same thing, neatness, do the seams all meet at the corner together, are they stitched the same width all the way around, in a quilt, are the stitches even, the same size, the same distance apart?

[Mrs. Kelly:] Do the colors blend, that go well with one another? Have the dark and the light all spaced.

Nothing should be too extreme a color or an inappropriate blend of materials. The garment should be suitable for its purpose; a playsuit should be made of sturdy washable fabric and allow freedom of movement, while a party dress should be cut softly with details that show care, effort, and some fragility. Uniformity of construction, purpose, and materials again rate high.

In crafts, although criteria essentially replicate those of needlework (neat workmanship, evidence of labor, suitable blending of colors and materials, item appropriate to use, nothing too extreme), the merits of originality and freehand design as opposed to copying or commercial reproduction are reflected in the debate between homemade and kits. In cooking, officials partly resolved this issue often by specifying that the exhibitors had to manipulate the cake mix in some way. Another partial resolution exists in the tacit admission that, while officials permit box cakes, they do not encourage them because scratch cakes taste better and show more work. In sewing, the concept of originality arises in the choice of colors, fabrics, and notions for a garment, but the originality must be within a strict framework of possible choices of appropriateness. A few needleworkers combine pattern parts to make their own personal pattern; this is considered laudable but, ironically, not always perceptible if well done.

One problem in crafts is that participants feel that they need a special ability, apparently somewhat different in quality from cooking and sewing, to design and execute hand-built pottery, decorative painting on wood like

Figure 5.5   Needlework pictures from kits, Ford County, Illinois

rosemaling, or rugmaking, as in latch hooking. In cooking they follow a recipe; in sewing, a pattern. But in crafts, the problem seems to be that a special, different, "artistic" ability is required to reproduce the many real-life models nearby.[2] Mrs. Fawcett and Mrs. Wilson expostulated:

> Kits, non-kits, it's costly to be original if you don't know design or haven't studied design or if it doesn't come to you naturally. Color, I've tried to be original but it doesn't look good to me when I'm done.

> You need an art course and a design course and a lot of things like that, probably. . . . Yeah, you have to have a talent.

> Well, in decorative painting, how many people can sit down and draw a group of strawberries or a group of daisies or something like that and have it look, not stilted? You know, have it look like something.

Craftspersons prefer kits in some cases because they are clean, fast (an attribute especially favored by women working outside the home or with children), and realistic. Most women and men, except for judges with some art school training, regard freehand or homemade efforts as somewhat pathetic unless they look very polished. As one woman remarked: "The ones with no kits, they might have thought up their own ideas, you know, which might not have looked as terrific, but still is worth having a category for."

As in photography and floriculture, tension sometimes arises between some judges with "art" training and some competitors. The competitors usually prefer judges who are working photographers, craft store workers, or who are from the Agricultural Extension Service. They feel these people's values stand closer to their own. Originality (irregularity, roughness) and homemadeness are not reviled in crafts; they are merely qualities secondary to others, such as realism, smoothness, and straight lines.

Horticulture, fruits, and vegetables follow the same pattern as the other departments. In corn, one looks for uniformity of the ear and straightness of the row. The tips and butts of the ear should be filled out, with no cob showing if possible. Long, full kernels make more corn for seed. The kernel should be bright and rounded to show the amount of oil and freshness.

Judges evaluate forage grains by weight per bushel. They look for very clean seed, with no foreign materials, insects, or weed seeds. They seek freshness; nonfresh forage grains look dull and have insects. Hay should smell fresh, not musty; the bales should have uniform squares and should be a bright color, with no rain spots on them.

Judges evaluate vegetables and fruits on edibility, which subsumes other criteria like size, quality, uniformity, freshness, texture, and color. Mark Hawley said, "Well, quality, and how much they look alike, you wouldn't enter a great big one and then a little one. You want three that are uniform and then you have to think about the food value—how much are you going to get out of it." Largest does not imply best at all. Largest, in fact, often indicates that the edibility would be lessened because the taste and texture are not as fine as in the smaller produce. Vegetables must be mature, but not too mature. What the public would buy in the store, what the public prefers, supplies the basis of evaluation here. No soft spots, no scabs, and no woodiness. The color should be characteristic of the variety of fruit or vegetable. Appearance provides the first set of traits for judgment in horticulture; if that does not suffice, the judge will cut open an item and judge on texture and perhaps even on taste. Ripeness or greenness, shape and size, and especially uniformity furnish the criteria for horticulture.

Figure 5.6   Straight and full ears of corn, Ford County, Illinois

While still in the plant category, floriculture judging sets standards that are definite and seemingly somewhat different from those in horticulture. As in crafts and photography, some division exists between floriculture judges with a formal art or flower-arranging background and those who are actively employed in the field or who judge on the basis of experience. Professional or avocational flower arrangers usually follow ideals and rules that are not necessarily compatible with the goals and standards of the fair population. Therefore, as in arts and crafts, the officials try to hire judges who reflect and actualize their constituents' values. These values do not ignore basic tenets of flower arranging or garden club rules. The county fair merely accentuates different points of specimens and of flower arrangements. The state university and 4-H clubs contribute criteria also, so that the floriculture criteria synthesize all of these sources and take the individual into account.

Crucial factors here include balance and rhythm as in other departments. Rebecca Jones commented: "You may have a little bouquet that's just real round. Okay. So there's rhythm there, even though it doesn't go this way or that way." She implies a distinction here between garden club and county fair flower criteria. Plant and flower arrangements that require "line" (definite direction) are not popular because entrants find them difficult, time consuming, a little messy, and the results do not match the decoration in most houses. As Christina Barron, floriculture superintendent said:

> Garden club arrangements are different from fair arrangements. . . . garden club are line with two or three flowers and a lot of whirligig things . . . that's not for the fair, that's garden club. Some are close [at the fair] like driftwood, but garden club are fancy arrangements, everybody tries to see who can get the most exotic-looking one. . . .
>
> Fair arrangements are more wholesome, they have a little more stalk to them. . . .
>
> . . . it's flowers for everyday living, 'cause any one of these centerpieces you could put on your table, you could put them in your home and there'd be a place for them, where a lot of garden club things, you'd have to have a lovely special table, special furniture.

In specimens, judges look for form in the flower to see the presentation, front and back. They look for straight stems, insect or spray damage, per-

Figure 5.7   Blue-ribbon arrangement, Ford County, Illinois

fect shape and matching petals, a center that is properly placed in the middle, and, in a collection of specimens, uniformity. The judge will take weather and location into consideration, but only for the group, not the individual entry. As in horticulture, the flowers should be at the peak of freshness, and this involves some tricky manipulation of timing for fair season and duration.

The list that has emerged indicates that the judgments embrace a community-based set of accords, more concerned with harmony and proportion than idiosyncratic variability.[3] This set emphasizes the celebration of the essence or prototypes of exhibits rather than the aberrational or the avant-garde. The critical vocabulary of positive visions of the entries that has emerged indicates three levels of concern within this critical process: substance, relationship, and use.

"Substance" takes in such terms as *fast, muscle, lean, rangy, straight, strength, capacity, structure, tall, angular, chiselled, clean, clear, smooth, fine texture,* and *fine line.* All these terms describe prospects of physical form. These terms describe one sole facet of the object under scrutiny, without reference to other characteristics or objects.

Under "relationship" I place *uniformity, eye appeal, balance, harmony, soundness, correctness, good, bad, characteristic, typical, firmness, rhythm, ripeness, not too much, not too little, symmetry, consistency, evenness, average, blended, proper, trueness, economical, lack of extremes,* and *placement.* These deal with abstract relations, especially among elements and among objects. They comprehend characteristics that are not tangible, yet are a matter of perception. They are concerned with combinations of characteristics that comprise the quintessence of a category.[4]

"Use" generally encompasses terms such as *efficient, cleanliness, freshness, edibility, appropriateness to function, purpose, like nature, purebred, homemade or personally manipulated in some fashion, suitable, lots of work involved, neatness,* and *realism.* These terms apply to external assessment of values outside the fair. They do not describe qualities of items themselves, or relations between items, but relations between the everyday world and items.

The substantive terms employ direct nomenclature in referring to their objects.[5] They develop practically no mediating metaphorical dimension or indirect description. The terms of abstract relationship employ more oblique approaches and metaphor. They point out the proper order among things, evolving concepts of material life along with metaphysical life. The third set of terms discerns social and cultural orders. They point out the proper relation between things people make and social values.

All these considerations of aesthetic description contribute to the metaphysical set of values with which participants invest their lives through the evaluation of their own work. Criteria for all the major departments of the fair show a remarkable consistency from category to category. The vocabulary and judging procedure reveal a relationship. Much the same structures for evaluation exist in similar fashion from livestock to flowers. Such agreement among departments, and among criteria, categories, choice of judges, physical, temporal, administrative, and historical structures argues a systematic set of values throughout the county fair. Aesthetics is more than just criteria, it is a set of interrelationships of values and judgments visible in many parts of the fair.

Patrons establish consistent criteria that celebrate middles rather than edges, consonance rather than dissonance, and symmetry rather than caprice. The ideal aspires to an incarnation of a type. Creation of an orderly progression from the particular (physical characteristics) through the metaphysical (relationships) to the general community life (external use) is a cooperative effort.[6] Originality, irregularity, and idiosyncrasy are acknowledged and accepted, but they are not rewarded in the same way that uniformity, harmony, and "proper relationship" are. From this base of stability, fair exhibitors, judges, and patrons may reach out to innovation and creativity as they do in the physical and temporal sections of the fair and as they do in the making of categories. Experiments with plant and animal genetics, food combinations, new technologies, and fabrics and patterns develop with a secure base. However, by the adoption of this analytical process, competitors reveal that their primary concern is to create the best possible example of that which they have chosen to produce. They want to ensure that they know the rules and opinions and techniques that will provide them with models for the best mode of living. From the concreteness of their work they formulate a set of mental criteria that they then utilize in their everyday lives.

Chapter Six

Working Aesthetics in Everyday Life

Green-bean canners and cattle breeders do not confine their judgments to the separate sphere of the fair; these judgments operate in participants' economic and social lives. The criteria help regulate economic activity in the region where they are developed. These criteria also facilitate social life by providing a basis of evaluation and a set of rules for personal interaction. Aesthetics literally works for this population in specific contexts with specific functions.

Economic Dimensions

During discussions of economic relationships it became clear that, in the context of the fair, participants' sophisticated understanding of multifaceted economic life in America receded in importance for them in favor of a more direct supply-and-demand, community-responsiveness model. Among other considerations, this model reduces the influences of the larger national domain on the fair and its surrounding community. The fair then gains in significance by regulating a more intimate, controlled association of economics and aesthetics. Even more significantly, the fairs show criteria in action, the criteria worked out in practice and connected with concrete concerns.

Livestock constitutes a department of major importance to the county fair. The breeding and raising of livestock are not as tightly organized on a large scale as is the growing of grain. The fair furnishes a welcome arena for airing commercial livestock concerns. Criteria for livestock discussed at the fair impinge on two segments of livestock culture: the breeding of animals and the production of animals for food. Judgments exercised at the county fair acquire a real measure of influence on the development of a breed. Livestock breeders do not develop these decisions in the abstract for the fair and then ignore them for other purposes. These decisions assume continuous significance for economic activity. Ed Luseby gave a good example of the kind of weight a county fair decision may carry concerning a beef cattle breed:

> We went to the county fair at Champaign County and I judged the county fair out there and you know, I particularly put up this one because he was tall, clean, and not very much fat on him, and he was thick. . . .

> . . . and suppose that it was, one of the popular ones today is Kianina, make it tall, long, and all of that sort of thing, and this is the one that I put up that I thought was the best that day,

> Well, everyone sitting around there, you know, the kids sitting around, the dads sitting around, they say, "well, this is the trend. Next year I'm gonna get me one like that."

> That's going to be the kind they use. This is what influences the selection of them.

The breeds develop in certain ways partly because of the decisions pronounced and promulgated at the fair. Animal raisers exercise enough judgment about the judgments (in most cases) to decide which are too extreme and which indicate the future direction of the breed. As Dr. Dodd put it:

> If you're going to be a breeder and if you're going to compete in shows, you have to be a judge. You don't have to go out and judge [professionally], but you have to be capable of discerning the kind which are acceptable. . . .

A lot of people work with cows all their lives. They don't have any desire to judge cattle. They might be quite competent, they just don't care to.

Yet every time you buy one, you're judging her. You make that judgment whether you want her or not.

And if you have purebreds, every time you sell one, you ought to be able to appraise her and know what she's really worth.

So you're judging her. And the guy who's buying her is judging her.

Most livestock breeders cite production of food as the primary reason for the breeding of animals in this part of the country. When farmers establish and accept the criteria for breeding animals, they do so with an eye toward what kind of meat or dairy products the animals will produce. One man in a crowd of exhibitors said that in particular the champion animal in any section would attract buyers because of the prestige and glamour associated with it. But the actual breeder of an animal for meat responds to the criteria that made up that champion and pays attention to the fairs as the showcase for what these criteria look like in the flesh. In a passage from his article "Fifty Years of Progress in Animal Science, 1908–1958," L. E. Mathers points out that "stock shows during the past fifty years have proven to be the outstanding classroom or laboratory for the assimilation, coordination, and dissemination of information in the art and science of animal husbandry."[1]

Not only do those criteria affect the conduct of daily economic life, they derive from that daily economic life as well. They thus perpetrate a cycle or dialectic that matches the fair, the cycle of agricultural life. There operates a cycle of influence, with criteria shifting between consumer and producer to establish an acceptable balance in every epoch. William Beckman expressed his views:

A person just farrowing hogs for market would buy a breeding boar animal from someone who does show at the fair because their animals have been judged and should be reliable and buyers know who wins and who doesn't. . . .

I think fairs are more influential now, say in hogs, to training people to raise the kind of meat the housewife wants and that's what raising livestock is all about, food.

And if you raise a product no one wants, you're out of business.

Criteria preoccupy the consciousness of those who buy and those who sell. Buyers and sellers need to judge and to reach a consensus of opinion in order to effect an exchange. The ones who establish criteria are the ones who use them, and they do so in the understanding of who and what are affected by these choices. As David Spivak described the circle of influence:

> The consumer has a big input into what the judges are looking for. Because of what they buy. And because of the livestock buyer at the stockyards, they want this type because the consumer's going to want, this is what the buyer's going to want.
>
> Eventually this is what the breeder has to raise—and this is what the judge eventually is going to be looking for.

A whole section of criteria dwells upon the suitability of these judgments and of the object, animal, or foodstuff for use outside the fair. When Dr. Dodd and Robert Edwards outlined the criteria for a good dairy cow, they described all of the properties in the context of the animal's suitability to give a good yield of milk and to be able to breed more animals that would also give a good yield of milk. Spivak, Olmert, and Beckman all talked about criteria for hogs seriously and jokingly as developing from what consumers buy and eat ("right off the plate"). The same held true of sheep, where the quality of the meat underlay the purpose of judging, according to the Rogerses. When Ed Luseby talked about beef criteria, his opinions aimed at selecting an animal who would be the fastest gainer and thus the best producer of meat. Every characteristic that these authorities described when they talked about the beauty of an animal related somehow to an economic issue.

Criteria apply both privately and commercially to the raising of vegetables, grains, plants, and flowers. Community opinion determines private satisfaction to some extent and has some effect on the consensus of criteria in turn. This takes on added importance when one considers the private or individual role in growing and arranging flowers, choosing or preparing vegetables, or planting and feeding grain to animals. As with livestock, however, there exists the commercial, public portions of these activities as well.

Florists' shops in the region often become a source of judges and models for proper flower specimens and arrangements. Florists and greenhouse operators and seed merchants conform to a certain extent to what they perceive as community bent. The heads of floriculture at the Sandwich and Champaign fairs are or were florists. An assistant at the Sandwich Fair had worked in a florist's shop. Other florists attend the shows and get ideas for their stores. In one fair the judge of herbs operates an herb store, farm, and greenhouse. She said there is constant exchange between herb journals, colleagues, and what they see at the county fairs and other shows.

The fair offers a kind of marketing survey of standards as well as pure education. Pictures in the catalogs should match growers' conceptions of plants and flowers. If homemakers do not feel comfortable with an arrangement in their home, they will not buy or make it. Florists know what to buy and arrange because they develop a place to help compose the criteria and to observe these criteria in action.

The evaluation of grains at the county fair allows farmers, operators of grain elevators, and salesmen to evaluate the correct quality of a product with some explicit guidelines. As Dr. Dodd pointed out in the judging of livestock, those who buy and sell grains must be able to understand the community consensus of good and bad grain in order for them to be a success in their occupations. Those who raise animals maintain interest in the best feed to make the best meats or milk. Grain raisers want to sell it. Grain brokers hold a stake in knowing the criteria that both those groups want. The fair helps to establish these criteria.

Vegetables raise many of the same issues. Grocery store produce buyers, seed catalog firms, and fruit and vegetable stand operators rely to some extent on the criteria negotiated between consumer, judge, and producer in order to make satisfactory commercial bargains. Only when they reach agreement can some sell and others buy. Negotiators reach those agreements and publish the results at the fair. When the Hawleys employ businesspeople to be judges and assistants in horticulture, they gather all the concerned elements together.

The production and consumption of food as a commercial venture depends on the comprehension of standards on the part of sellers and buyers. When restaurants serve food in the region, much of their menu reflects the people's opinion of what constitutes good food and how it should taste. When judges and exhibitors discuss the qualities of perfect bread, canned beans, or chocolate cake, those opinions find their way into the eating houses of the surrounding countryside. Restaurant owners know better than to ignore the expressed views of their customers. They sometimes can alter or add to the community's criteria to a certain extent. In general they engage in a process of synthesizing cultural and commercial tastes and the

Figure 6.1   Prizewinning wine from Napa County Fair, Chicago, Illinois (photo by Brian Rusted)

taste that satisfies the eater. Quite often some of the more successful county fair exhibitors become cooks and florists' assistants in town. They have shown themselves to be the quintessence of what the community desires. They then bring those standards with which they won their blue ribbons to commercial premises and make another successful exhibition in a different sphere. For example, in the mid-eighties a Chicago wine store offered rows of display wine bottles with information about the high numbers of ribbons won at the Napa Valley County Fair. In the early nineties, two women selling lemon pound cake at the West Tisbury Farmer's Market, in Massachusetts, attached their Duke's County Fair blue ribbons for the product to their advertising sign on their truck.

Commercial activity and criteria accepted by the community buttress each other in the area of decorated cakes. Commercial ventures provide the recent technology and the innovations that private customers use in their

Figure 6.2   Grand champion frosted cake, Waukesha County, Wisconsin

home efforts. Practitioners follow the new ideas set out in trade magazines and cake-decorating stores and bakeries. Practitioners and customers may accept or reject the available choices, but those choices of colors, decorating styles, and techniques always influence customers' standards.

In turn, the exhibitors and judges at the county fairs make plain what they approve and disapprove, accept and reject. Like the bakers and canners, the champion and blue ribbon cake decorators reveal to the commercial world as well as to their neighbors what their peers consider to be the best and most beautiful cakes. After the fair, one often sees these cakes in the bakeries and in the grocery stores. They appear in celebrations for which buyers commission cakes from talented friends who win at the county fair. The influence operates in both directions, from store and magazine consumer to maker and consumer, and from maker and consumer back to the commercial world. In both directions, the establishment of a consensus of criteria paves the way for action.

Raw materials, such as animals, seeds, and plants eventually become meats, vegetables, fruits, and baked, canned, and decorated goods. The decisions as to what constitutes "good" food depends on local interests' physiological and visual taste. Since many people are involved in the producing, buying, or selling of food, a local vision of a healthy economic life incorporates a local understanding of the nature of "good" food and its components. The same holds true for flowers, plants, and other crafted items, like clothing, photography, and basketwork. The making and judging of those things relate not only to competition at the county fair but to use in year-round life.

Craft stores and catalogs have been cited as sources for criteria and ideas. In turn, craft stores in particular extend antennae to pick up the standards and preferences for execution exerted at the county fair. Their customers encompass those who show at the fair. Some craft stores go so far as to exhibit prizewinning exhibitors' work in their windows, especially if prizewinners used materials from those stores to create their masterpiece. Even if not, a blue ribbon quilt or piece of macrame on display will prompt observers to go in to buy the materials to make one for themselves. The proprietors of such stores know their customers and their customer's county fair records. Many times the items popularized by their customers will be the basis of the next order of materials from the craft catalogs or distributors.

Commercial photographers who work in studios and newspaper offices give their opinions as judges and by example, but they also take their cues from the kinds of pictures their customers indicate they want at the fair. At the fair, ordinary viewers' assessments of groupings, subjects, and styles follow those of good judges for the photographs. Those that win are, in almost every case, those that demonstrate understanding of the relation of what someone makes to everyday usage or familiar situations.

Together with the criteria, the fair itself—and especially judging and exhibiting at the fair—acts as a force in participants' lives. Economic activity swells because of participation in the fair, not only because the criteria incorporate part of the commercial enterprise, but because the fair presents opportunities for advertisement, exposure, and experience. The fair carries social and psychological implications, too. The original mandate for the fair involved education and economics. County fairs have affected various parts of exhibitors' work and leisure with that mandate.

Those showing purebred livestock in the county fair consider advertising of goods a prime consideration. The breeders who show their animals increase the chances that their stock will become known and respected, especially if the animals win. Ed Luseby said that the idea of the fair is to "show the animals, to advertise, and to sell them high." When people exhibit their animals, they keep their ribbons already won visible in their hip pockets. Back in the stalls and pens, signs dangle above a breeder's animals or are pinned to the side of the enclosure. These signs proclaim the name of the owners, the name of a farm or breeding concern, and the place (usually the town) where they can be found. Alongside these signs often hang the array of ribbons a particular animal or farm has collected. Sam Warren, at the Sandwich Fair, said,

> It's the advertising value they get out of winning. . . . if they've got a good animal that's won prize after prize after prize, then it's enhanced its value in the livestock-breeding industry. So that's where he gets his gain. . . .

> The premiums just help with the overhead, transportation, having someone to help them at home while they're showing or at the fair.

The selling of animals at the fair forms another economic factor. Although advertising leads to sales, sometimes those sales are down the road in time. But breeders may sell a prizewinning or likely looking animal to a dealer or a hopeful breeder on the spot. The displaying of animals in the show ring affords a prime opportunity to advertise wares that may be taken home immediately. Frank Weaver added to Sam Warren's summary of commercial motivations for showing at the fair:

> The fellow that's in it is in it, and the fellow that's out is out.

> The fellow in open show is a professional, pure and simple, a breeder. . . . he's there partly for the ribbon because he hopes to cut his expense . . . but I don't think he expects to make any money.

> But he's there because he's a professional breeder and he's looking for exposure.

Exposure will certify exhibitors as professionals, active in the field, testing their animals against those of other livestock raisers and against public opinion. Exposure says, "Here is my product. I think it is good enough to be judged." And implicitly, bought.

Figure 6.3   Advertising at the county fair, De Kalb County, Illinois

Advertising at the fair functions in other areas than livestock. Businesspeople in the seed corn companies take advantage of the exposure they obtain by participating in the judging and exhibition section of the fair. As the Hawleys pointed out, the seed companies are the only outfits that sell seed corn. Farmers raise corn for human consumption from the first-growth corn. They then might sell corn on the market for cornmeal; corn flakes; cattle, chicken, and hog feed; mush; corn syrup; sorghum; and oil—all from second-growth corn of the seed corn sold by the companies. So by sponsoring the seed corn at the fair and providing a contrast within the grain exhibits, the seed companies benefit in their business dealings with the farmers, who will then buy it and raise second-crop corn. As Thomas Hawley said, this is a very real benefit:

And the judge picks the first, second, and third over the whole show.

And that first over the whole show gets the corn cup that the association buys.

And they'll use it. "First" at the Sandwich Fair.

The seed companies use the fair as a vehicle for exposure of their product, and the fair benefits from the denser, more plentiful exhibits that result. Those seed companies view the fair as a marketing and testing site and reap the rewards that accrue from winning. Mark Hawley said:

> Hybrid corn seed companies and research companies are expensive competition, each trying to outdo the others.
>
> We started the hybrid corn show . . . buying seed from a list of companies who then buy the premiums. One company doesn't want to be left out—usually we have to make room for more. It's good advertising for them.
>
> People come in just to look at it. When the judge works, he doesn't know which is which company. . . . they use this in their advertising.

This process also demonstrates community involvement of the seed companies, a good public relations move. It illustrates commitment to the processes the local population finds important. Still, while the fair furnishes a venue in which companies pursue some of this advertising and public relations, these activities do not compare with the winning of a "blind" competition judged by an impartial adjudicator. In expression of values combined with public relations, they do not compare with the visible results on display, grown by farmers participating in the program.

County fair activity and professional growth within the county fair often produce an impetus for economic success outside the fair. Those who formerly had avoided professional activities because of timidity or lack of expertise have benefited, sometimes inadvertently, from their hobbies that became livelihoods. Some florists, photographers, bakers, and seamstresses not only have used the criteria exposed at the county fair but began their business careers because of their successes at the county fair.

For instance, some women began sewing and arranging flowers for private use and enjoyment, and their work caught viewers' eyes while it was on display at the fair. Potential customers then asked if they would work for others, making quilts and clothes for neighbors and friends for pay. The same goes for flower arrangements. In some cases when fair patrons have certified that a person possesses talent that appeals to members of a community, neighbors invite her or him to grow or arrange flowers for weddings, churches, funerals, and other events.

Bakers and cake decorators alike have discovered the fair to be an important stimulus to their professional lives. Paula Hornlein told two stories of bakers who were launched on careers by participation in county fairs. One woman had been a champion baker:

> We had a woman over here in Oswego who entered the layer cakes in particular and she's very excellent.
>
> And of course she was involved in 4-H for years and years.
>
> And now she's helping in the kitchen of a tea room over in Oswego.
>
> I was in there a month ago and there were some women at the table next to us and it was interesting. They were talking about her and the fact that she's the one that used to enter these cakes at the fair and won all the blue ribbons.
>
> People remember those things.

Another woman found that the county fair competition revealed a rich source of customers for her cake-decorating skills. She had entered a decorated cake and it was duly displayed at the fair:

> They got this first prize and lots of time people take the names and addresses off of those (entry cards) and then they will basically contact them at home, even if they are not professionals. . . .
>
> We had one cake last year that was a fishing creel, it was the basket and it was beautiful work and of course, when you decorate cakes, and you make the effect that it is woven in and out like a basket would be, this was beautiful, the lid was standing up. . . .
>
> And everybody took the name and address of the woman because they were thinking about their husbands and brothers and their sons and she makes those in two or three sizes.

Paula Hornlein said this woman got a lot of orders from the cake she exhibited, although neighbors did not consider her a professional.

In photography, the members of a family who had won many prizes turned their hobby to good account. They won all the prizes up to Grand Champion. After that, they did not enter in the fair any more. They instead became the photographers for events in the De Kalb area. They had become accomplished and well known through the county fair.

In all these cases, the development or internalization of criteria that the community sanctions and appreciates helps the participant to lead an effective local economic life. People have indicated here that they must have some connection and understanding of a judgment or item if they are to accept it into their lives. If the items have no place in participants' scheme of things either because they are unfamiliar with them or because they go against their taste, they reject them. Exhibitors express the need for harmony both as a criterion for their products and as a criterion for their everyday perceptions. They do not have one set of values for art and another for life.

The creation of the county fair best reflects the criteria of balance, harmony, consistency, consensus, display of abilities, room to experiment with unfamiliar forms within a known and controlled context, and display of neat, hard work. As social action, the economic dimension of the fair permits nothing too extreme, usually a result of consensus, but does permit trials for innovation. At the Sandwich Fair, officials talked about different projects that people had opposed or adopted. Someone will propose an idea and then they will discuss it. Mr. Weaver said, "Most of the time, if it looks reasonable, we'll say let's have a shot at it." Mr. Warren added:

> It keeps the interests of the different superintendents and their departments. If you say no every damn time they want something . . . you go out on a limb and try it just to prove they're wrong or right.

Rather than bringing in outside professionals to run the fair, local community members in Illinois regard the fair as their own homemade, purebred product. They allow commercial activity by others within the precincts of the fair, but they would rather use the talents and participation of the neighborhood.[2] They attempt to establish an accord that will make patrons feel pleasurably part of an enterprise, and that will produce an enterprise worthy of the community. They pay attention to concrete characteristics in order to build the fair's ethos in accordance with their everyday lives.

Social Dimensions

The structure of the fair and its criteria also apply to social existence. The preferred mode of social intercourse for medium to large numbers of colleagues and neighbors develops through a cooperative effort. People very much enjoy potluck suppers because everyone participates and no one person carries the economic or social burden of entertainment. When Sam and Louisa Rogers hosted the annual lamb dinner for their shepherd colleagues and friends (whom they had met largely through exhibiting sheep at the county fairs), everyone brought a dish. Not only did everyone bring a dish, but the dishes were discussed by some guests beforehand. Guests commanded one woman to bring the group's favorite taco salad; they were disappointed when she brought something different one year. People have arranged, after some experience, to maintain a balance of greens, starches, salads, and sweets to go with the lamb. Guests revel in interesting combinations of familiar and unfamiliar ingredients.

Like the lamb supper, and like the county fair itself, a celebration in honor of the outgoing president of the Ford County Fair was a community-based effort (the community in this case being those connected with the county fairs) in which everyone contributed time, effort, or expertise. One set of people constructed an exhibit, another set made the invitations, another made the food, and yet a fourth set decorated the fair office at the fairgrounds, where they held the party. People dressed properly, as for other social events I attended in east central and northern Illinois. "Dressed properly" meant in accordance with local dictates of propriety discovered at the fairs. I perceived a certain uniformity and harmony between fabrics, demeanor, and food. No one laughed incessantly or too loudly, started a fight, came dressed in blue jeans or gold lamé, or roasted hot dogs in the middle of the cake and pie buffet. The cores of activity retained their identity, and social consensus led guests to consistent expressive forms and behavior.

Illinois county fair goers divide responsibilities in the conduct of a church bazaar, Home Extension meeting, or folklore interview in the same way that they show cooperation in their criteria. In the number of group interviews that I conducted, there was little interruption, and everyone was given an opportunity to speak about what he or she knew best. Each person also received time to speak about subjects that were not his or her specialty.

An even tenor with only occasional aberrations characterized the interview conversations.

The social use of criteria manifests itself in gift exchange and home occupations as well as in events.[3] First of all, the categories that surface at the county fair are the same categories of items exhibitors choose to make during the year. When the church bazaar opens in the fall, the classes of goods for sale parallel those at the fair. When one is received as a guest in this region, handiwork hangs on the walls, stands on pedestals, or rests on furniture. Visitors view afghans, embroidered or patchwork pillows, macrame plant hangers, wooden brackets, latch-hook rugs, and painted wood or tin in neighbors' homes. These things function as decorations because people give them as gifts and because they use them to enhance their own rooms.

Gift exchange becomes quite important here. For the same reason that friends bring food to one another's houses, cultural rules impel them toward the making and giving of other things, especially crafts. Part of the reason involves economics; just as it is cheaper to have everyone share the expense of entertainment, so they also make rather than buy presents. Also, in food and gifts, giving something the donor values shows the value of the recipient. That criterion, which Thomas Hawley stated as "one's very best vegetables are anything you would put on the table if you had the best of company," shows the honor in which social relations are held and how material goods express those social relations. The making and giving of presents, like meals, affirms shared values and a spirit of cooperation in building a home in the same spiritual if not physical neighborhood.[4] The making and giving of craft gifts sets up an opportunity for donor and recipient to offer and accept a gift of a kind of value that both sides can appreciate. The criteria have been specified for good workmanship: pleasant blending of colors and materials and amount of work involved. Those party to the transaction are aware of the nuances. They understand the specified function and evaluation of an object and the intent of the donor. Even if they do not know ultimately what to do with it or if they do not like it, they still can appreciate its aesthetic and thus social significance. The gift links them by symbolizing shared understandings.

Objects one has made enhance one's own environment when those objects satisfy maker and user or viewer. One method by which they become a source of satisfaction is that of judging and exhibition, which allows people to estimate the object's importance in a system of values. Once

Figure 6.4   Pillow at home, De Kalb County, Illinois

this has been accomplished, then the object and its environment acquire worth, because they have been judged and placed. When they have been judged and then placed (in a competition, in a physical setting, and in a system of values), people have established a relationship with their objects within an environment. When most of these things have been created by self, family, or friends in an effort that includes attempted adherence to shared judgments of taste, then the satisfaction deepens. By exhibiting the results of the making process, the makers place themselves in public, relating themselves to others on moral principles, principles of how to live in a social world.

One of these principles is that of cleanliness. The concern with neatness, propriety, and uniformity gains social and philosophical importance in agricultural communities, where so much of one's life and livelihood depends on forces of nature uncontrollable by humans. People's lives connect with dirt, soil, refuse, excrement, weather, and death more intensely than do the lives of average suburban dwellers. People bring sustenance as well as order from this chaos. However, it is not surprising that a preoccupation with forces of order, balance, and cooperation, evident in the county fair

Figure 6.5   Scarecrow sculpture, Carroll County, Illinois

criteria, should dominate. The concern with cleanliness and symmetry in the things humans make or raise tempers the dirt and chaos of the external natural world:[5] "[T]he division between cleanliness and filth, purity and impurity, is that between Christian and pagan, the civilized and the savage. . . . Chadwick . . . asked 'how much of rebellion, of moral depravity and of crime has its root in physical disorder and depravity.' "[6]

For this reason, flower arrangements that go off in all directions or look messy, as Christina Barron earlier remarked, are not acceptable because they merely replicate existing conditions. They do not give much perspective on their environment or reassurance for people who live so close to what those arrangements represent. A cleaving to well-defined forms such as roundness and fullness rather than spiky spareness cushions residents in their farms and provides a companionable feeling. The coolness or extremely controlled chaos of garden club arrangements does not suit county fair participants because they value neighborliness and consensus in order to cancel out the isolation and randomness that are still features of agricultural life. They do not want arrangements that jar with existing decorations or furniture styles.

County fair participants currently prefer recognizable pictures and photographs, designs, and categories as antidotes to the abstractions and ambiguities of nature, among other reasons. In a world in which dirt and tornadoes control much of their livelihood, they use the security of a firm, familiar core in order to venture out. They live in a different social, economic, and physical world from that of citizens whose aesthetic preoccupations emphasize risk and ambivalence.

The significance of art, if analyzed as degrees of removal and definitions of relationship through human creation, whether livestock, quilts, sculpture, or painting, becomes a matter of cultural context rather than absolute pronouncements.[7] The people who assist in creating aesthetic judgments and who feature them at their county fairs are the people who have demonstrated their consistency and applicability in year-round living.

Chapter Seven

Festival of Art and Aesthetics

When I first started thinking about county fairs in connection with the creation and evaluation of art, I wondered if *art* was a term that would be used only by an outsider. Would the conjunction of *art* and *county fair* sound ridiculous or incomprehensible or irrelevant to the participants in the judging and exhibition sections of the fair? In America, we often assume that there can be no relation between what appear to be such diverse institutions as a county fair and an art gallery.[1] The only negative responses I received on the subject, however, came from academic colleagues, one of whom said after hearing about the project, "Pigs is pigs," and another who said, "There's nothing aesthetic about county fairs." Aesthetics, and art, have been hoarded as resources belonging to a very few residents of this country. They form a province in which only the elite may vacation. Alan Merriam directly addressed this issue in saying:

[I]n discussing the aesthetic, Western aestheticians have made it applicable to but one kind of art. In so doing, they have strengthened the division made in our culture between "fine art" as opposed to "applied art" or the "artist" as opposed to the "craftsman" . . . it is a culture-bound concept applied by us to those particular forms which we call fine art.[2]

Criteria that include a belief in art for art's sake characterizes the dominant concept of aesthetics in American art (derived from nineteenth-century European romantic aesthetic philosophy).[3] Currently influenced by romantic notions of the primacy of feeling and spontaneity and the significance of the individual, many aestheticians, critics, and arts administrators tend to extol the primacy of formal analysis and the contemplative, nonfunctional model as the ideal. They seem to assume that all art is removed and elevated from ordinary life and concerns, and that genius makes art. Art lives on the edges and in the vanguard or avant-garde of achievement.[4] Robert Hughes represents a cadre of commentators when inveighing against multiculturalism in art on the grounds that it produces "little that might, in aesthetic terms, challenge, refine, criticize, or in any way extend the thinking of the status quo."[5] Genius, novelty, and innovation are celebrated. This is one kind of aesthetic but only one. It seems as though individuals with influence in the "arts" regard it as though it is *the* only one.[6]

The danger of this attitude is that it excludes all other endeavors from being considered "artistic." These judgments are not only culture bound but class and era bound. In fact, what has happened is that the aesthetic to which county fair participants largely subscribe derives from eighteenth- rather than nineteenth-century models. Cartesian rationalism comes into play in the emphasis of county fair categories on the usual and familiar rather than the extreme and, indeed, on the precise calibration of those categories; in the reliance of the judging procedures on appropriate rules; and in the focus of the criteria on elements such as absolute representation of the qualities of a category, typicality, harmony, uniformity, everything fitting together, and balance.[7] Of course other elements enter the picture, but the aesthetic involved substantially favors a century earlier than the one that influences dominant and influential cultural commentators today. Ironically, what was once the hallmark of elite culture now, two and a half centuries later, represents folk thought in America. Because they subscribe to an earlier aesthetic, many Americans do not conceive of themselves as artists, as competent evaluators in the realm of creation, or even as having any relationship to art whatsoever.[8] Most people's self-image concerning art assumes that someone else measures up to the tacitly standard national system of aesthetics, not they. Then they are excluded from a large arena of self-approbation and appreciation, an arena with merit in the eyes of society. Art and aesthetics confer a high value on those who practice the craft or profess the theory. Many citizens become shut out from what is popularly called the cultural life of our nation.

Another danger of only one nationally applied set of aesthetic criteria is that a relatively exclusive group of practitioners—teachers, curators, scholars, writers, arts administrators, and patrons—become the arbitrators of this aesthetic. Whatever group currently holds power determines the nature of the aesthetic, what phenomena may take their place in this system, and what changes will be permitted.[9] Thus art and aesthetics have both been removed from the ken of the world at large. Who *does* get to articulate social values through aesthetic judgments? In Lawrence Levine's description of the culture wars of the late 1980s, he characterizes those "aficionados of any cultural genre . . . [who believe] that the sun shines brightest in their own cultural backyards."[10] Politicians and administrators tend to allot money, performance and exhibit space, art education, and political attention on the basis of a system that implies a very particular view of life and that admits only one notion of value to its ranks. Although Levine was optimistic that the boundaries of culture had widened, the escalation of the war to control the National Endowment for the Arts in the early 1990s belies his optimism. There is nothing wrong with any one notion of value, only that it pervades standards to the point of ignoring the existence of other kinds of judgments and arts.[11] Taste is linked to identity. And therefore, as Kenneth Ames says of historical artifacts, with implications for the present:

> It is intellectually irresponsible to continue to unreflectively confer the honorary degree of art on a small segment of the artifactual world of the past blithely ignoring most of the surviving artifacts because they do not measure up to an unstated but implicit canon of acceptability.[12]

Unlike the construction of the currently dominant framework of artistic judgments, which most of us only passively assent to or dissent from, those who participate in the county fair, partly because of its folk nature, help to elaborate and articulate a series of critical judgments. With the help of thinkers like Ed Luseby, I have designated these judgments and their collective nature as aesthetic processes. *Aesthetic* in this case refers to theories of taste, especially the critical evaluations concerning things material or perceptible to the senses. The processes by which county fair participants construct the criteria that are the bases of the judgments are processes of aesthetic determination. They are those processes that determine the beauty or value of sensual and material objects to the appropriate community. Their set of aesthetic processes is a vital force, because these are shared processes that participants apply to the familiar things of daily life and integrate into their everyday lives. They reveal through the county fair what they find pleasing in their day-to-day activities, and how they express and utilize those judgments. They make their own aesthetic system, and they use it.

Art refers to human constructions as opposed to the constructions of nature. Building on George Kubler's suggestion in *The Shape of Time*[13] that we call art those things that people make, I modified that somewhat to: Art here is the human reordering of elements of the mental or physical environment according to significant canons of judgment, allied with affect, deliberation, and/or thought in order to provoke, to perceive or reperceive something, or to comment on some aspect of life.

While it is true that most people I interviewed or observed did not bring up the terms *art* or *aesthetics* themselves, they had no problem with the concepts once I had broached them. Clearly, Ed Luseby, in his quote about the combination of art and science producing progress in discussing criteria, was already with where art fit in the scheme of raising, showing, and judging cattle. It was I, like my academic colleagues, who assumed that art and county fairs would of course remain mutually exclusive. However, county fairs, along with those things participants produce or raise and then exhibit there, can lay claim to residence in the realm of art.

The institution of the fair acts as a distillation of and a comment on the daily rounds of life. It provides the arena for the formulation and expression of the standards that support action in the social and economic community surrounding the fair. As well, the fairs display and exhibit the work of their constituents. These institutions expose their skill and mastery and act as opportunities to show off and examine the competition. Mrs. Kelly said:

I think you think about workmanship. . . . I think you sort of notice.

It's competitive, to be neat and to learn how to do different things. And then, when you get together with your friends, you talk about, oh, how'd you do that and this and that?

And then being in Home Extension, we get lessons on all those things and you just pick it up as you go along.

> I think you try to compete with the other fellow and have your stitches look good.

Display and exhibition distill and reorder as well. Mrs. Hodge mused:

> They've made this at home, the only time anyone else sees it is when they come into their home, so why not bring it out and show it to everybody? Which is good.

> I think people get really good ideas. Like, other people might not have even thought of doing any of these, you know, so if they see something at the county fair, they might think, that's really nice and go home and maybe look into it.

> I think that's how I got excited about doing crafts, seeing the nice things.

Intensification aids this distillation and reordering process. The proliferation of items focuses attention on the objects. The increased population participating in the exhibition intensifies human awareness—adds significance. Because this jar of string beans leaves the more prosaic kitchen environment and arrives at the exhibit case where it demands attention, it receives scrutiny and value that comes from surprise. In effect, the county fair recontextualizes everyday life through the exhibition process. It takes work out of one place into another and by this act requests a new kind of notice. That notice in turn grants consciousness to the work within the home, barn, or studio. As Mrs. Kelly said, "I think you try to compete with the other fellow and have your stitches look good."

Officials exhibit work in such a manner as to satisfy the needs and values of artist and audience. The county fair superintendents follow patterns of culturally determined beauty in judging what and how they display artifacts. The Hawleys discussed display aesthetics in the same careful manner that parallels the consideration of a gallery curator organizing a show:

> We don't line all of the same things in one spot, we change it all over. . . .

> You mix all the colors up so it looks pleasing rather than having all of your red in one place and all of your green in another. . . . But if you set each one by itself, intermix them, . . . never put two greens together, two yellows together. . . . we keep our classes together. But between our yellow beans and

our green beans you might have some red tomatoes or white onions or something. . . .

You want to set it up in the building so that when somebody comes and gets inside that door, they go "Oh!" They can't imagine anything that looks like that.

County fairs provide a small, intensified reordered world that isolates and focuses the aesthetic system. Within this artistic world we find pieces of art. What people make reorders one's environment and perceptions in manageable fashion. It is not a reproduction but a re-presentation of elements that signify meaning and perception to an individual and to the collective judgment of a community.

The fair recreates the world, but in a more controlled, formal incarnation. In this way we manipulate our environment for the kind of illumination that the alternation of patterns vouchsafes to us.[14] This enables artists and audience to pause from unconsidered or mundane views of the art or artifacts in order to contemplate other values of the work. An exhibition such as one finds at a county fair discloses the nature of the decisions by which concerned patrons judge that art. Through this exhibition process, fair officials separate items from an ordinary, complex context.

Community members articulate meanings through the judging system. An art gallery presents these meanings according to one set of aesthetics and the county fair according to another. The nature of the aesthetic may take different forms and be built on different assumptions, but the notion of having an aesthetic is shared by both worlds and deserves respect and contemplation.

Festival shares many characteristics with art. The agricultural fair celebrates a way of life. It is a festival of people and occupation and region and imagination. Sam and Louisa Rogers told it this way:

You see, we talk about how other people do things, and you make friends that you have the rest of your life. They're often interested in the same things we are, and they're from different parts of the country and it's a friendship that sticks a long time.

Here fairgoers welcome the chance to participate in the unaccustomed company of others. They trade opinions and share the excitement that a crowd generates. Other elements combine to augment the excitement: the

Figure 7.1   Re-presentation of farming, Winnebago County, Illinois

smells of many stands of hot dogs and candy apples joining with the odors of unusual livestock barns; the shouting, calling, and laughing of barkers, announcers, and friends at the fair in resonance with the poignant carousel music of the midway and the blare of the motorcycle races on the track; the glinting sun on metal trucks and striped canvas contrasting with piles of manure and the shadowy interiors of the barns and the exhibit halls—all manufacture a carnival of the senses. In the judging and exhibition sections alone, the sheer volume of entries arrests the attention of a person used to looking only at his or her own pantry, closet, garden, wall display, or barn. In the Sandwich Fair crafts section, the supervisors counted 104 throw pillows entered in 1980. Describing the intensification of humans and objects, Mrs. Fawcett and Mrs. Wilson of the Crafts Department said,

> We have probably twelve, fourteen people [working for us]. It takes that many to get things out Tuesday night [before the fair].

> Some just work Tuesday night for three or four hours, four or five hours. We have all these pictures to hang, three or four hundred pictures.

Walking down barn aisles the observer confronts row after row of tails and eyes of numerous breeds of livestock.

Celebrants gather to focus attention in a positive fashion on agriculture and rural life. The Latin root of celebrate *(celebrare)* means to go in great numbers to honor someone or something. Annually, participants hold a festive commemoration of the raising of food and the activities connected with it, loosely interpreted. Groups respectfully mark their everyday lives through the ritual exhibition and judging of their work. Special sets of behaviors, ceremonies, and rewards initiate an atmosphere of paradox and therefore command attention: intensity and drama with lightheartedness and hard work with vacation. William Beckman gave this interpretation:

> I guess it's recreation. I was told once it's a plowman's vacation. . . .

> . . . it's just something people like to do, instead of playing golf at night you would walk hogs or wash them and do all of those different kinds of things—it's the desire for competition.

Visitors eat strange foods and, as Ed Luseby explains of his own fairgoing, visit with seldom seen friends and neighbors:

> I like to go to the county fairs, see the animals other than the cattle being judged, look at the animals in the barn if there's no judging going on, see some of the breeders, see trends, other judges, and I'll talk.

> Some of my best friends will be there, some of my excellent friends.

They act in unaccustomed ways in order to pay homage to their lives and to their comrades who make those lives possible. In order to do those things, they invite strangers to judge them, to bring entertainment, and to operate dislocating carnival machines to emphasize by contrast the stability of their everyday lives. Bright colors, exciting sounds, sweet and fat tastes, and a variation from routine all imply good times.

This intensification and presentation to outside gaze allies with forcefulness. It fixes an event in a scheme of importance. County fairs are intensified experiences. They take place in a circumscribed place and time, encompassing a wide range of activity. Smells, sights, and sounds concentrate and magnify. The unusual number of human beings collected in one place, engaged in similar concerns, also intensify the experience. Intensification pulses in the preparation immediately before the fair. Exhibitors and fair officials described a flurry of activity preceding opening day. Last-minute completions, alterations, and details increase the pressure and thus the awareness of work for special occasions. The preparation of items for exhibition adds to the proliferation of events, which together proclaim significance and compel attention. This assault on the senses vividly colors experience and marks it indelibly in the blood.

The fair encompasses other events, such as concerts, variety shows, races, dances, amusements, rides, eating, competitions, and socializing. The fair also detaches itself from everyday life. It occurs once a year, for a specific period in a specific place. The fair creates a separate world with its own rules, personnel, and expectations. It possesses a special recognizable character of "fair." This character organizes life in a particular fashion separate from ordinary living, yet with components of life similar to the big world. It combines elements of the concerns of social and economic life with play, replicating forms of usual existence.[15]

The festival mien of fairs partly explains why the aesthetic judgments promulgated there mean so much in revelers' lives. These qualities aid in propelling important psychic products of the fair into mental and physical action during the year. Positive connotations of merrymaking and entertainment often attach themselves to a festival. County fairs in the Midwest perform diverse functions aided by these distinctive features that characterize festivals and that imprint experience onto human consciousness.

The qualities of festival serve to catapult social and economic standards and evaluative thought systems into life outside the fair. These qualities assist the fair to function both as exemplar and as a site for experimentation with alternatives. Since the fair provides a good time, participants associate good times with the work and values that are exemplified at the fair. They associate good times also with experimental alternatives that are presented at the fair in the guise of parody and strangeness. Participants respect and enjoy the "serious" categories and judging procedures, but they love the atmosphere of vacation and revelry in which it is set. The "play" categories and entries, the unusual foods, the fellow carousers met on the midway—all indicate alternative modes of living and thinking that both reinforce and alter life as participants know it. The fair operates both as a conservative and a dynamic force in the yearly cycle.

One of the ways in which the fair retains its vividness and thus its impact year round comes through the fact of preparations.[16] Exhibitors keep criteria in mind in preparing to exhibit their work. Preparation constitutes a long-term, continuous preoccupation. Because it exists throughout the year, the significance of the fair exists throughout the year. The importance of the fair then invests that year-round work with increased significance. Louis Olmert said:

> There's a lot to it, when you get to thinking about it. While you're doing it, you get so you realize . . . it just is daily work but every year you prepare.
>
> If you want something to show the next year, you got to do certain things at certain times during the whole year round to make sure you're ready for next year's fair.

Preparation for the fair highlights ordinary work. The fair focuses what might otherwise be diffuse routine occupation.

The fair wields influence in other spheres along with occupational life. Fair activities enrich family life. Often the impetus for involvement in the fair comes from family connections or relatives who ask others to help out. When relatives help each other they reinforce ideas about family solidarity. Inhabitants in this region feel strong blood ties; the fair activity gives them the chance to test these ties. Philip Clarke mused:

> My son was practically raised up at the fair.
>
> I remember one time when the carnival was setting up down here, they had a young boy about his age. He let this other boy tie him up and we had to go rescue him. That's how little he was when he started following the fair.
>
> And then he got to be fair electrician and had the sound system.
>
> And he does a lot of other work, too. We impose on him. Because who else you going to grab out and get to do some of the jobs that need to be done?

Those who grew up with the fair generally stay with the fair. Not everyone within a family, of course, wants to participate or continues participating after they become adults. But a large number do maintain their connections with the fair work. The influence of the fair on generations holds as much significance for exhibitors as it does for officials and workers. Many commentators have remarked on how family members across generations continue to participate as a unit. Paula Hornlein said:

> In our 4-H club, two of the mothers entered the fair when they were first married, and now their kids are coming in with some needlework or some cooking, there are some who enter as families yet.

> Mother enters and maybe a brother's got some livestock, we have three or four 4-H families in our area alone who come over to the fair and enter probably in six or seven different areas.

Significantly, families participate as families at the fair; this activity encourages them to act as families during the year. Mrs. Kelly described her family interaction for the fair, first with her mother and then with her daughter:

> I used to come and deliver [flowers] for her, that was my job. She'd pick them the night before, and she'd arrange them the next morning. . . .

> Then Eleanor was in 4-H, and that girl would take umpteen projects. . . .

> . . . and I had to help her a lot and to always press on with your project and get that knitted dress done.

Exhibitors learn the skills and value judgments from each other. They revel in the anticipation in preparation for the fair. Common goals and tangible aid enhance their interaction as a family unit. Preparation for fair week helps them reassure themselves that they are indeed important to each other. That importance flowers at the fair itself. Just as community members determine their social and economic significance to each other, using the aesthetic standards they have evolved and awarding prizes and holding dinners and events, so do family members see the results of their year-round labor and inculcation of beliefs at the fair.

County fairs enhance memory as much as they foster anticipation. Many conversations focus on the fair as a reference point, either as a source of stories, a repository of humorous occurrences, or as a stimulus for pride in achievement. In many houses I saw trophies from the county fair dis-

played. I also saw displays of ribbons hanging in different rooms. Participants give prominent positions on the walls to arrangements of the photographs of awards being given and received, or prizewinning animals or
products, or family groups at the fair. Many people keep scrapbooks of pictures, newspaper articles, and other memorabilia of the great week. Ribbons and photographs glow from their patterns arranged under glass. Many
times, inhabitants cluster these mementos in a special room, usually an office or workroom of some sort. Here these items remind their owners and
visitors of festival work or achievements at the fair in a way that connects
with their everyday lives. These concrete reminders of pride and happiness
shine on the owners' daily efforts. Mrs. Kelly told of one person who ex-
emplifies making this kind of relation between her work and the fair: "The
lady who comes and stays with my mother does a lot of crocheting and
when you walk in her house, she has a big picture up on the wall, and all
around, she has her ribbons pinned up on that big picture. So she's really
proud of those ribbons." And by association, of her crocheting.

Those who keep scrapbooks look at them often. These constructed
collections of memories form a coherent picture of an identity forged by
and with the county fair. The books concretely establish the record of personal achievement and involvement. They recall the less tangible but
equally potent mental and emotional identifications stemming from the
county fair and the successful interpretation of community criteria. In fact,
participants use these mental and emotional identifications of self and community with criteria at the fair year round in the same way that they associate criteria with year-round action. The distillation of year-round action
into significant celebration at the fair in turn distills into memories through
associations, ribbons, trophies, pictures, and objects hallowed by participation in the county fair.

Those memories then serve as the basis for further action leading to
the fair and so on into the kind of symbiotic cycle that predominates in
agricultural life. People then perceive examples of reinforcement and alternatives that the festival of the fair highlights as possibilities for action during the year. Jane Turner expounded this function to me:

> I also go for ideas. . . . I think it's fun to see what other people come up
> with, whether maybe it's a kit I've seen in a magazine but haven't seen
> worked up yet or if there's ideas of their own, how they drew it out and
> then executed their plan whether it'd be needlepoint or . . .

Figure 7.2   Trophy display at home,
De Kalb County, Illinois

Figure 7.2   Trophy display at home,
De Kalb County, Illinois

... the different things that are available and just see if there're any new
ideas and sometimes there are things that maybe I could do, maybe we
could use them for our church bazaar.

The separation of human creation and judgment of that creation from routine life by the reordering power of festival (art) invests these examples
with a power that might not be otherwise recognized.

Participation in the aesthetic processes of the county fair often provides a domain of control and personal significance that other realms of life
lack. Competition and the chance to win ribbons play an important role in
proving self-worth for future endeavor. Mrs. Fawcett told me:

And another thing, when we were entering, it was fun to see how we compared, we liked our work to a certain extent, but then we didn't know how

good we were, so it was fun to take it and if we got a blue ribbon, it gave us
a little more confidence to go on. . . .

I've seen people *grow* in their work.

The fair constitutes one of the few organic institutions where peers present
their work and their ideas to their neighbors and receive those opinions in
turn. The aesthetic system in the county fair shows the real import of people's mental and physical control over their own work and mind.

The maker exerts control over his or her physical environment by
combining elements in a fashion that makes sense to her or his world. The
judge exerts control over his or her own cognitive environment through
evaluation of those combinations. Reordering, taking elements from one
place and reemphasizing them or recombining them so that human makers
engender emotions and ideas, occurs in the judging process. It also occurs
through the conscious construction of one's world. The human mind or hand
creates significance knowable by humans. In the county fair, exhibitors create significance about ordinary people, not startling exceptions or singular
events. When a breeder reorders a cow through genetic engineering or a
quilter rearranges shapes of material, and when their peers judge these
items, the local community celebrates appropriateness to function, symmetry, harmony, uniformity, vividness, and quintessence of categorical form,
middles rather than edges. Participants move from the concrete, highlighted facet of physical form through abstract relations and perceptions of
quintessential form to external values outside of the fairs. The judgments
connect up the whole range of their experience in a coherent way.

The fair is an alternative world made up of artistic rearrangement of
elements that exist in the regular world, but not in the same form. Structure
is a system of relationships; the fair reemphasizes or recreates these relationships. Fairgoers eat, sleep, work, dispense justice, transact business, so-
cialize, build, entertain, and learn for a period of time within the confines of
the fair. The notion of an alternative, idealized world sets the life of the fair
apart from the life outside the fair in order that cultural principles may be
more clearly apprehended and constructed. We recognize the physical forms
of the "streets," buildings, and fields as those used in the everyday world,
but they intersect and unite in unusual ways. They have contiguities not obviously found outside the fair, especially in the orderly fashion by which
they are laid out at the fair. The fair brings out relationships that exist in a

more submerged way in everyday life. Fair spaces are representations of barns, exhibit space at home, and social areas. The physical aspect of the fair, like the temporal aspect, is a stylized version of space and time outside the fair. The legal system is similar in its assumptions of a hierarchical system of justice, but officials implement the system according to county fair rules.

The grooming and showing of animals, preparing items for show and arranging them, and social interaction are found outside the fair, but they are fashioned again within the fair. Showing and judging are shaped behaviors that are practiced at home in a routine manner for the exercise of the animals, for the decoration of the house, or the feeding of a family, but they are performed at the county fair in public in an ideal fashion. The ideal cannot be reached in real life because of innumerable restraints, but it can be approached at the fair because of its isolation and because it is the point of all other activity. People judge at home, but often privately, tacitly, untested by the community. At the fair, participants publicize those judgments and declare the rules for a social world, not an idiosyncratic world. The fair is art; it showcases art, embodies aesthetic principles, and acts as a forum for the development of aesthetics.

Participants use aesthetic criteria at the county fair to highlight significant elements of their lives. The creation and use of a system of judgments provides the power of discernment and thus a release to act. Judgment is action and judgment derives from everyday acts in this context. In the case of those involved with the Illinois county fairs, significant elements in their aesthetic are social and economic, just as in other cultures they might be religious, historical, environmental, or formal.[17] The nature of the aesthetic here is determined by its use in the community and the meaningfulness in context, as finally stated by a livestockman at the Champaign County Fair:

Well, you talk about beauty.

I was walking with a young woman from Chicago and we stopped to look at some wheat fields. It was the end of the summer and they were full of wheat.

And she said to me, look at that, all golden and shining. Isn't that a beautiful sight? Isn't that pretty?

And I said, yes, that's certainly pretty. But that would be more beautiful in my eyes if that field of wheat were scythed and stacked into sheaves.

That would be a beautiful wheat field.

Notes

art does not have to be idiosyncratic to be art.

Introduction

1. I have been to fairs in Wisconsin, Iowa, New York, Maryland, and Pennsylvania, and I have heard contemporary descriptions of fairs in Mississippi, Oregon, Vermont, and West Virginia. Academic and literary descriptions in the works listed below convince me that a certain amount of generalization is permissible. Wayne Neely, *The Agricultural Fair* (New York: Columbia University Press, 1935); an essay by Joyce Ice, in Delaware County (New York) Historical Association, *Farm Work and Fair Play* (Delhi, N.Y.: Delaware County Historical Association, 1990); David C. Jones, *Midways, Judges, and Smooth-Tongued Fakirs: The Illustrated Story of County Fairs in the Prairie West* (Saskatoon, Saskatchewan: Western Producer Prairie Books, 1983); Warren J. Gates, "Modernization as a Function of an Agricultural Fair: The Great Grangers' Picnic Exhibition at Williams Grove, Pennsylvania, 1873–1916," *Agricultural History* 58 (July 1984): 262–279; Fred Kniffen, "The American Agricultural Fair: The Pattern," *Annals of the Association of American Geographers* 39 (December 1949): 264–282, and "The American Agricultural Fair: Time and Place," *Annals of the Association of American Geographers* 41

(March 1951): 42–57; Lila Perl, *America Goes to the Fair: All about State and County Fairs in the USA* (New York: Morrow, 1974). The literary works that follow cover fairs in specific states. Vermont: Dorothy Canfield Fisher, "The Heyday of the Blood," in *Hillsboro People* (New York: Henry Holt, 1915), pp. 37–49; Michigan: Della T. Lutes, "The County Fair," in *The Country Kitchen* (Boston: Little, Brown, 1935); Iowa: Ruth Suckow, *Country People* (New York: Knopf, 1924), pp. 79-80; and New York State: Laura Ingalls Wilder, "The County Fair," in *Farmer Boy* (New York: Harper and Brothers, 1953), pp. 252–275.

2. Neely, *The Agricultural Fair*, pp. 61–62.

3. In his article "On Appreciating Agricultural Landscapes" (*Journal of Aesthetics and Art Criticism* 43 [Spring 1985]: 301–312), Allen Carlson makes a case for a relativist vision of new criteria for judging new environments.

4. See Hunter Thompson, *Fear and Loathing in Las Vegas* (New York: Random House, 1989), for a description of gonzo investigation and the mentality that prompts it.

5. For a description of the factors leading to distinctions and separations between farm owners and farmworkers, see Peter H. Argersinger and Jo Ann E. Argersinger, "The Machine Breakers: Farmworkers and Social Change in the Rural Midwest of the 1870s," *Agricultural History* 58 (July 1984): 393–410.

6. Of course, the VCR and shopping malls now play big parts in social life and entertainment as well. Many people specifically cited the county fairs as deliberate moves away from the loneliness of the television set.

7. The issues of power and authority in ethnography and cultural production have been initiated and explored by James Clifford, *The Predicament of Culture: Twentieth-Century Ethnography, Literature, and Art* (Cambridge: Harvard University Press, 1988); James Clifford and George E. Marcus, eds., *Writing Culture: The Poetics and Politics of Ethnography* (Berkeley: University of California Press, 1986); Richard G. Fox, ed., *Recapturing Anthropology: Working in the Present* (Santa Fe, N.M.: School of American Research Press, 1991); George E. Marcus and Michael M. J. Fischer, *Anthropology as Cultural Critique: An Experimental Moment in the Human Sciences* (Chicago: University of Chicago Press, 1986); Eugene W. Metcalf, Jr., "From Domination to Desire: Insider and Outsider Art," in *The Artist Outsider: Creativity and the Boundaries of Culture*, ed. Michael Hall and Eugene W. Metcalf, Jr. (Washington, D.C.: Smithsonian Institution Press, 1994); Edward Said, *Culture and Imperialism* (New York: Knopf, 1993); and Trinh T. Minh-ha, *Woman, Native, Other: Writing Postcoloniality and Feminism* (Bloomington: Indiana University Press, 1989).

8. See, in particular, Trinh T. Minh-ha's discussion of difference and identity in *Woman, Native, Other*, particularly in the chapter "Difference: A Special Third-World Women Issue," pp. 79–116. This problem of otherness and specialness is by no means simple; she presents its ambiguities well.

9. Brett Williams, anthropologist, American University, and Warren Belasco, cultural historian in American Studies, University of Maryland, Baltimore County.

10. George Judson, "Fair Celebrates an Imperiled Way of Life," *New York Times*, August 28, 1993. Nik B. Edes brought this article to my attention.

The Aspect of the Fair

1. For a related view of this, see Néstor García Canclini, *Transforming Modernity: Popular Culture in Mexico*, trans. Lidia Lozano (Austin: University of Texas Press, 1993); Canclini says, "However, we do not go so far as to tell which are the elements [of fiesta], present in all symbolic production, that involve the invention of new realities, games about reality, and openings, or windows, to what is not or to what we cannot become. How can we understand these refutations of reality that we keep on constructing in the palaces of the world of dreams, in utopian and literary archetypes, in the profitless expenditure of a fiesta, in every strategy of the imaginary realm and the rhetorical tricks of desire?" (p. x). Garcia Canclini speaks of oppositional creations here but also the same functions of reordering reality for commentary as art as I perceive in the county fair.

2. These quotations from fieldwork interviews are given without formal citation of date, place, and individuals' true names to protect their privacy. The interviews all took place in northern and central Illinois and southern Wisconsin between 1980 and 1982. In the quotes, the material in brackets is from the interviewer—usually my questions.

3. See ibid., pp. 87–92, for a discussion of folk culture and degrees of community involvement in traditional and urban fiestas. The midwestern county fair seems to encompass the whole range within one celebratory structure.

4. Gaston Bachelard, *The Poetics of Space* (New York: Orion Press, 1964), p. 150.

5. Cf. Victor Turner's well-known thesis of liminality stated in *The Ritual Process: Structure and Anti-Structure* (Ithaca, N.Y.: Cornell University Press, 1969), pp. 94–130.

6. See Roger Abrahams, "Christmas and Carnival on Saint Vincent," in *Western Folklore* 31, no. 4 (1972): 275–89; Robert Jerome Smith, "Licentious Behavior in Hispanic Festivals," *Western Folklore* 31, no. 4 (1972): 290–98.

7. I am indebted to Fred Kniffen's suggestions in personal communications and to writings of other cultural geographers and anthropologists for methodology and ideas here. In particular, I found helpful James Agee and Walker Evans, *Let Us Now Praise Famous Men: Three Tenant Families* (Boston: Houghton Mifflin, 1960); Mary Ann Caws, ed., *City Images: Perspectives from Literature, Philosophy, and Film* (New York: Gordon and Breach, 1991), esp. pp. 33–70; John Collier, Jr., *Visual Anthropology: A Research Method* (New York: Holt, Rinehart and Win-

ston, 1967); esp. pp. 77–104; Edward T. Hall, *The Hidden Dimension* (New York: Doubleday, 1966); Daniel Kemmis, *Community and the Politics of Place* (Norman: University of Oklahoma Press, 1990); Howard Stein and William G. Niederland, eds., *Maps from the Mind: Readings in Psychogeography* (Norman: University of Oklahoma Press, 1989); and Yi-Fu Tuan, *Topophilia: A Study of Environmental Perception, Attitudes, and Values* (Englewood Cliffs, N.J.: Prentice Hall, 1974) and *Space and Place: The Perspective of Experience* (Minneapolis: University of Minnesota Press, 1977).

8. These categories come from my own observation, reading of the maps and premium books, and interviews with participants in the fair. When I used them in conversation with other fairgoers, the categories appeared to match most peoples' perceptions of the fair.

9. A passage written by Fred Kniffen in 1949 still effectively summarizes the installations of today's midwestern fair: "The pattern of the fair consists of two parts: a set of permanent installations; and a group of ephemeral structures, erected and removed with each active season. The permanent part of the pattern was distinguishable in its modern form by 1870. Then as now it consisted primarily of fence, track, and grandstand with barns, sheds, and halls varying in number and quality with the size and financial status of the individual fair.... The most striking changes in mass effect are part of the temporary pattern, above all the replacement of acres of horse-drawn vehicles by relatively much larger areas of parked automobiles and the appearance of trailer camps as successors to the tent camps of an older era. On the other hand, the tent street of the midway has changed little since its acceptance late in the nineteenth century" ("The American Agricultural Fair," p. 282).

10. Ian Starsmore, *English Fairs: Studies in Industrial Archeology* (London: Thames and Hudson, 1975), p. 23.

11. In "Modernization as a Function of an Agricultural Fair," pp. 262–79, Gates convincingly discusses the commercial section of agricultural fairs (and thus argues for the whole fair) as the site of exposure to new ideas, machines, political developments, and thus modernization.

12. Starsmore, *English Fairs,* p. 96.

13. See Edward Braithwaite, *Fairground Architecture* (London: Hugh Evelyn, 1968), and Starsmore, *English Fairs*.

14. "This is eulogized space. Attached to its protective value, which can be a positive one, are also imagined values, which soon become dominant. Space that has been seized upon by the imagination cannot remain indifferent space subject to the measures and estimates of the surveyor. It has been lived in, not in its positivity, but with all the partiality of the imagination" (Bachelard, *Poetics of Space,* p. xxxi).

15. Kniffen, "The American Agricultural Fair," and Karal Ann Marling, *Blue Ribbon: A Social and Pictorial History of the Minnesota State Fair* (St. Paul: Minnesota Historical Society Press, 1990).

16. Marling, *Blue Ribbon*, p. 185.

17. Quoted in Richard K. Matthews, *The Radical Politics of Thomas Jefferson: A Revisionist View* (Lawrence: University Press of Kansas, 1984), p. 39. Leo Marx, in his *The Machine in the Garden* (New York: Oxford University Press, 1964), demonstrates the tenacity of this viewpoint in America.

18. Susan Stewart, *On Longing: Narratives of the Miniature, the Gigantic, the Souvenir, the Collection* (Baltimore: Johns Hopkins University Press, 1984), p. 128. In Gaston Bachelard's terms as well, people have before them a miniaturized world. The difference is, the observers are the ones who have miniaturized it and who have helped design it. Through this activity, the fair people experience what Bachelard does when he says: "The cleverer I am at miniaturizing the world, the better I possess it. But in doing this, it must be understood that values become condensed and enriched in miniature" (*Poetics of Space*, p. 150). He quotes a *Dictionary of Christian Botany*'s (1851) discussion of flowers, remarking that detail increases an object's stature (p. 154).

Historical Constructs/Administrative Constructions

1. William Addison, *English Fairs and Markets* (London: B. T. Batsford, 1953); T. F. G. Dexter, *The Pagan Origins of Fairs* (Cornwall, England: New Knowledge Press, 1930); Alessandro Falassi, *Time Out of Time: Essays on the Festival* (Albuquerque: University of New Mexico Press, 1987); Raymond Muncey, *Old English Fairs* (London: Sheldon Press, 1925); Ellen Moore, *The Fairs of Medieval England* (Toronto: Pontifical Institute of Medieval Studies, 1987); Neely, *The Agricultural Fair;* Starsmore, *English Fairs;* and Cornelius Walford, *Fairs, Past and Present: A Chapter in the History of Commerce* (London: Elliot Stock, 1883).

2. Dexter, *The Pagan Origins of Fairs.*

3. Walford, *Fairs, Past and Present,* pp. 3–4.

4. Sir Henry Maine, cited in Addison, *English Fairs and Markets,* p. 3.

5. David Braithwaite, *Fairground Architecture* (London: Hugh Evelyn, 1968), p. 14.

6. Addison, *English Fairs and Markets,* p. 25.

7. F. C. Roope, *Come to the Fair: The Story of the British Fairgrounds and the Showmen Who Attend Them* (London: "The World's Fair," for the Showmen's Guild, 1962), p. 101.

8. Great Britain, Ministry of Agriculture and Fisheries, *Markets and Fairs in England and Wales* (London: H.M. Stationery Office, 1927), p. 9.

9. Dorothy Davis, *Fairs, Shops, and Supermarkets: A History of English Shopping* (Toronto: University of Toronto Press, 1966), p. 11.

10. Braithwaite, *Fairground Architecture,* p. 17.

11. Roope, *Come to the Fair,* p. 9.

12. Ben Jonson, *Bartholomew Fair,* ed. Edward R. Partridge (Lincoln: University of Nebraska Press, 1964).

13. Davis, *Fairs, Shops, and Supermarkets,* p. 243.

14. Joan Thirsk, ed., *Chapters from the Agrarian History of England,* vols. 2, 3, and 4 (New York: Cambridge University Press, 1990); E. L. Jones, *Agriculture and the Industrial Revolution* (Oxford: Blackwell, 1974).

15. J. V. Beckett, *The Agricultural Revolution* (Cambridge, Mass.: Basil Blackwell, 1990), p. 17. Beckett suggests that the most critical development for agriculture between 1760 and 1830 in England was the spread of new techniques and their widespread adoption. He mentions that it took time to persuade farmers to use new practices and years before they became fully effective. Similar concerns characterized American agricultural development. In the case of England, the example of the landowners in addition to the exhibitions helped; in the case of America, later in the nineteenth century, the fairs assisted in the promulgation of the techniques, as well as the creation of peer pressure.

16. As Jane Tompkins suggests in *Sensational Designs: The Cultural Work of American Fiction, 1790–1860* (New York: Oxford University Press, 1985), "when these principles are enacted in a fiction, rather than being enunciated abstractly, they have the power to excite emulation."

17. Beckett reminds us, however, that a sizable amount of the credit should go to the lesser landowners, tenant farmers, and agents, who worked hard and constantly for improvement of agriculture. *Agricultural Revolution,* pp. 28–29.

18. Neely, *The Agricultural Fair,* p. 39.

19. "Leading the Movement for farm improvement during the period from 1790 to 1860 was a group of gentleman farmers, or agriculturalists, who experimented with improved techniques of farm management and communicated their discoveries in agricultural periodicals, farm books, addresses, and other published media" (Paul G. Bourcier, " 'In Excellent Order': The Gentleman Farmer Views His Fences, 1790–1860," *Agricultural History,* October 1984, p. 546).

20. Richard K. Matthews, *The Radical Politics of Thomas Jefferson: A Revisionist View* (Lawrence: University Press of Kansas, 1984), p. 46. Matthews points out that "Jefferson tries to introduce decentralization into virtually every facet of life; not wishing to see these scientific agricultural societies centrally controlled from the federal capital, he persuasively argues for local jurisdiction," thus setting the scene for county fairs along with state or national exhibitions.

21. Neely, *The Agricultural Fair,* p. 47.

22. Ibid., pp. 61, 62.

23. Ibid., p. 62.

24. See the historical literature and literary works already cited, and Alan G. Bogue, *From Prairie to Corn Belt: Farming on the Illinois and Iowa Prairies in the Nineteenth Century* (Chicago: University of Chicago Press, 1963).

25. Here are just a few of the contemporary sources that do not mention county fairs: Eliza W. Farnham, *Life in Prairie Land* (New York: Harper and Brothers, 1846); William Oliver, *Eight Months in Illinois, With Information to Immigrants* (Chicago: Newcastle upon Tyne, 1843; repr., Walter M. Hill, 1924); James Stuart, *Three Years in North America*, 2 vols. (Edinburgh: Robert Cadell, 1833); and Alexis de Tocqueville, *Democracy in America*, 2 vols. (New York: Harper and Row, 1966).

26. Neely, *The Agricultural Fair*, pp. 82, 85.

27. Warren J. Gates, "Modernization as a Function of an Agricultural Fair: The Great Granger's Picnic Exhibition at Williams Grove, Pennsylvania, 1873–1916," *Agricultural History* 58 (July 1984): 277.

28. Ibid. See also Julie Ann Avery, "An Exploration of Several Early Michigan County Fairs as Community Arts Organizations of the 1850's and 1870's," vols. 1 and 2 (Ph.D. diss., Michigan State University, 1992); Felicia Romano McMahon, "Wilderness and Tradition: Power, Politics, and Play in the Adirondacks" (Ph.D. diss., University of Pennsylvania, 1992); and Carolyn Hope Roston, "To Make a Better Spirit: Community and History at the Hill Town Fairs of Western Massachusetts" (Ph.D. diss., University of Pennsylvania, 1993).

29. Neely, *The Agricultural Fair*, p. 89.

30. Ibid., p. 193.

31. Much of the information came from Neely, *The Agricultural Fair*, p. 135. One important discussion of the extension service can be found in Jim Hightower's *Hard Times: The Failure of the Land Grant College Complex* (Washington, D.C.: Agribusiness Accountability Project, 1972). For other views, contact the Director of Communications, Information, and Technology, Extension Service, Department of Agriculture, Washington, D.C.

32. Jane H. Adams, "The Decoupling of Farm and Household: Differential Consequences of Capitalist Development on Southern Illinois and Third World Family Farms," *Society for the Comparative Study of Society and History* 30 (July 1988): 453–82.

33. See Peter H. Lindert, "Long-run Trends in American Farmland Values," *Agricultural History* 62, no. 3 (Summer 1988): 45–85, esp. 70–85, for a discussion of recent capitalization practices on farms and how they may have affected or been affected by the general economy.

34. Gates, "Modernization and the Agricultural Fair," p. 268.

35. Kniffen, "The American Agricultural Fair."

The Premium Book Categories: Charting Relations of Value

1. Claude Levi-Strauss, *The Savage Mind* (Chicago: University of Chicago Press, 1966). See also F. G. Asenjo, *In-Between: An Essay on Categories* (Washington, D.C.: Center for Advanced Research in Phenomenology and University

Press of America, 1988); Dan Ben Amos, ed., *Folklore Genres* (Austin: University of Texas Press, 1976); Brent Berlin, *Ethnobiological Classification: Principles of Categorization of Plants and Animals in Traditional Societies* (Princeton, N.J.: Princeton University Press, 1992); Pierre Bourdieu, *The Logic of Practice* (Cambridge, England: Polity Press, 1990); Mary Douglas, *Purity and Danger* (New York: Praeger, 1966), and *Rules and Meanings* (Baltimore: Penguin, 1973); Michel Foucault, *The Order of Things: An Archeology of the Human Sciences* (New York: Vintage, 1973); Gary Gossen, *Chamulas in the Land of the Sun* (Cambridge: Harvard University Press, 1974); Nancy Munn, "Visual Categories: An Approach to the Study of Representation Systems," in *Art and Aesthetics in Primitive Societies*, ed. Carol Jopling (New York: Dutton, 1971); and Rodney Needham, *Symbolic Classification* (Santa Monica, Calif.: Goodyear Publishing Company, 1979).

2. Henry Glassie, "Meaningful Things and Appropriate Myths: The Artifact's Place in American Studies," in *Prospects* 3 (1977): 1–49; Dan Ben Amos characterizes systemic meaning in *Folklore Genres,* p. 225: "It is a qualitative, subjective system of order. The logical principles that underlie this categorization . . . are those which are meaningful to the members of the group and can guide them in their personal relationships and ritualistic actions. . . . It is a self-contained system by which society defines its experiences, creative imagination, and social commentary." Also see John Borneman, "Race, Ethnicity, Species, Breed: Totemism and Horse-Breed Classification in America," *Comparative Studies in Society and History* 31 (January 1988): 25–51, on classifications legitimizing social concepts of race and ethnicity; Mary Douglas and David Hull, eds., *How Classification Works: Nelson Goodman among the Social Sciences* (Edinburgh: Edinburgh University Press, 1992); Mary Hufford, *Chaseworld: Fox-hunting and Storytelling in New Jersey's Pine Barrens* (Philadelphia: University of Pennsylvania Press, 1992).

3. The phrase is taken from Amanda Dargan, "Dividing Up the World: Strategy and Opposition in a Form of Speech Play" (paper presented at the American Folklore Society, Los Angeles, October 1979).

4. In a conversation with me in 1981, the folklorist Claire Farrer remembered a time in the 1960s when she went to a county fair in New Mexico to look at quilting methods and was disappointed not to find any quilts there for reference.

5. Warren Belasco, conversation in 1992.

6. 28th Annual Carroll County premium book, Mt. Carroll, Illinois, 1980, p. 11.

7. They often increase the variety of cucumbers (gherkin and dill), tomatoes (cherry and catsup), peppers (banana and hot), and squash (crookneck, acorn, butternut, buttercup, and Hubbard). Various sorts of cabbage and potatoes and strings beans swell these ranks. Superintendents also add on pumpkins, brussels sprouts, and less common produce like leeks, shallots, and garlic.

8. Ford County Fair premium book, Melvin, Illinois, 1980, p. 138.

9. Carroll County premium book, p. 29.

10. Greater Champaign County Fair premium book, Urbana, Illinois, 1981, p. 55.

11. Carroll County premium book, p. 28.

12. Ford County Fair premium book, p. 141.

13. Douglas, *Purity and Danger*.

14. Brian Sutton-Smith and Elliot Avedon, *The Study of Games* (New York: Wiley, 1971).

15. Sandwich Fair in De Kalb County premium list, Sandwich, Illinois, p. 65.

16. Sandwich Fair premium list, p. 21.

17. Sandwich Fair premium list, p. 75.

18. Ford County Fair premium book, p. 133.

19. Greater Champaign County Fair premium book.

20. Sandwich Fair premium list, p. 94.

21. Ibid., pp. 82, 89, 90.

22. Greater Champaign County Fair premium book, p. 56; Ford County Fair premium book, p. 141; Sandwich Fair premium list, 1980, p. 57.

23. Fairbury Fair premium book, Fairbury, Illinois, p. 71; Greater Champaign County Fair premium book, pp. 66, 70; Sandwich Fair premium list, p. 76.

24. Much as a department of classics or folklore does in a university that currently idolizes engineering. Many administrators regard classics and folklore as old-fashioned or frivolous or time-wasting, and yet diverse points of view, values, and problem-solving methods of these disciplines are essential to the well-being of the educational system.

25. See Cyril Smith, "Art and Technology" (address given at the University of Illinois, Urbana-Champaign, 1982); Cyril Smith, "Structural Hierarchy in Science, Art, and History," in *On Aesthetics in Science,* ed. Judith Wechsler (Cambridge: MIT Press, 1978), pp. 9–53.

"A Good Judge": The Ritual of Evaluation

1. Ronald Grimes, *Ritual Criticism: Case Studies in Its Practice, Essays on Its Theory* (Columbia: University of South Carolina Press, 1990); Frank Manning, ed., *The Celebration of Society: Perspectives on Contemporary Cultural Performance* (Bowling Green, Ohio: Bowling Green University Press, 1983). My discussion with Brian Rusted, a communications theorist at the University of Calgary, Canada, about these sources and cultural performance has been very useful.

2. Although there are many more recent works on performance and performance theory, Richard Bauman's article "Verbal Art as Performance," *American Anthropologist* 77 (June 1975): 290–311, remains the best source for explication; the terms on performance (though not the discussion on perform and show) derive from this article.

3. See J. O. Urmson, "On Grading," in *Logic and Language,* 2nd series, ed. A. G. N. Flew (New York: Philosophical Library, 1953), pp. 159–86; Carl Fleischhauer brought this article to my attention.

4. James Deetz, *Invitation to Archeology* (New York: Natural History Press, 1967), esp. pp. 43–101.

5. Richard Bernstein, *Praxis and Action* (Philadelphia: University of Pennsylvania Press, 1971) p. 19; also see Mary Douglas and Baron Isherwood, *World of Goods* (New York: Norton, 1985).

6. Aristotle, *Theory of Poetry and Fine Art,* with a critical text and translation of the *Poetics* by S. H. Butcher (New York: Dover, 1951).

7. R. O. Urmson, "On Grading": "even if an apple, *per impossible,* satisfied all the criteria which we require for good as an end and good as a means in the case of cabbages, it would not be a good apple. Though we have agreed that some criteria are less central than others, there still remains a hard core of criteria which have to be satisfied in each different case, which cannot be generalized into any one or two formulae. Why an apple which tasted like a good cabbage would certainly be a very bad apple we have not yet ventured to discuss, but a very bad apple it certainly would be" (p. 177).

8. In his *Anthropology: Culture, Patterns, and Processes* (New York: Harbinger, 1963), A. L. Kroeber discusses the relationship of individual and culture; see esp. pp. 94–103. See also Yi-Fu Tuan, *Segmented Worlds and Self: Group Life and Individual Consciousness* (Minneapolis: University of Minnesota Press, 1982).

"Eye Appeal"/Aesthetic Criteria for Judging

1. H. Sanders, *The Co-operative Extension Service* (Englewood Cliffs, N.J.: Prentice-Hall, 1966).

2. See Cathy Annette Brooks, "The Meaning of Childhood Art Experience: A Dialectical Hermeneutic" (Ph.D. diss., Pennsylvania State University, 1980). A good discussion of models and cognitive acquisition.

3. There is an interesting comparison with the Japanese aesthetic here. See, for instance, Soetsu Yanagi, *The Unknown Craftsman: A Japanese Insight into Beauty* (New York: Kodansha International/USA Ltd. through Harper and Row, 1981), and V. Hrdlickova, "The Japanese Professional Storyteller," in Amos, *Folklore Genres,* pp. 171–90: "Storytellers regard the mastery of these elements as a necessary stage preliminary to any successful practicing of their art in public, for the audience not only expects of them an established manner of interpretation, but also rates them according to the degree of mastery the artists command. For this reason, storytellers do not attempt to exhibit their individuality by overthrowing these principles but by gradual introductions, based on a command of the professional technique and minute oversteppings of the traditional framework."

4. Robert Plant Armstrong, *The Affecting Presence: An Essay in Humanistic Anthropology* (Urbana: University of Illinois Press, 1971), p. 19, usefully describes a concept of relations and experience: "All the forms, however, are characterized by relationality and experience. Relationality is intended to designate those relationships that come to exist among parts, either in time or in space. . . . Experience is a complex of elements relating to values, and it alone is the cause of that flash of relevance, that quality of illumination which makes of the whole work a valuable and significant documentation of human being."

5. Arthur Danto, *The Transfiguration of the Commonplace* (Cambridge: Harvard University Press, 1981), especially pp. 90–114 and 165–208, in which he discusses the relation of terms and their objects.

6. I am in the debt of Cathy [Brooks] Mullen for discussion of these problems and schemas, along with the exploration of the ideal and normative sections of judging.

Working Aesthetics in Everyday Life

1. L. E. Mathers, "Fifty Years of Progress in Animal Science, 1908–1958," *Journal of Animal Science*, 1958.

2. They do not always welcome the entire neighborhood, however. The Champaign County Fair featured a beloved African-American barbecue chef, but most fairs' visible participants remained overwhelmingly white and northern European.

3. See Ferdinand Tonnies, *Custom: An Essay on Social Codes* (Chicago: Regnery, Gateway Editions, 1971), and Marcel Mauss, *The Gift: Forms and Functions of Exchange in Archaic Societies* (New York: Norton, 1967). Also see David J. Cheal, *The Gift Economy* (New York: Routledge, 1988); Mary Douglas and Baron Isherwood, *The World of Goods* (New York: Norton, 1985); Caroline Humphrey and Stephen Hugh-Jones, eds., *Barter, Exchange, and Value: An Anthropological Approach* (Cambridge: Cambridge University Press, 1992).

4. "Standing back to view his work, the carpenter noticed how much more the house now seemed like those in the center of town. Although it stood in the middle of more than a hundred acres of farmland tilled by the Mott family, its new face would tell the people of Portsmouth that Jacob Mott was one of them, just as though he lived as their next door neighbor" (James Deetz, *In Small Things Forgotten* [Garden City, N.Y.: Anchor Books, 1977], pp. 2–3).

5. See Linda Borish, "The Lass of the Farm": Health, Domestic Roles, and the Culture of Farm Women in Hartford County, Connecticut, 1820–1870" (Ph.D. diss., University of Maryland, College Park, 1990), esp. pp. 246–319 and pp. 406–42, on the subject of the farm wife's historical preoccupation with dirt and cleanliness.

6. Peter Stallybrass and Allon White, *The Politics and Poetics of Transgression* (Ithaca, N.Y.: Cornell University Press, 1986), p. 131.

7. See Armstrong, *The Affecting Presence,* and G. Charbonnier, ed., *Conversations with Claude Levi-Strauss*, (London: Jonathan Cape, 1969).

Festival of Art and Aesthetics

1. Edward D. Ives describes the art common to peoples' endeavors in his *Joe Scott: The Woodsman-Songmaker* (Urbana: University of Illinois Press, 1978), using poetry as his subject: "I am not talking about 'natural context' or 'folk aesthetic' or anything of that sort at all. I am talking about what have been for me moments of great integrity, moments when I have been transformed. . . . They need no apology existing as they do in a place beyond understanding, where no tight smile or condescension can touch them. . . . And there, far from the enormous assaults of the universe, after the ultimate unjudgement of death, I will find Joe Scott and William Yeats drinking beer together in quiet and understanding" (p. 436).

2. Alan Merriam, *The Anthropology of Music* (Chicago: Northwestern University Press, 1964), p. 260.

3. My source for the discussion of eighteenth- and nineteenth-century notions of aesthetic thought is Monroe Beardsley, *Aesthetics from Classical Greece to the Present: A Short History* (New York: Macmillan, 1966). These characterizations were brought to my attention by Stanley Charkey, a composer and musicologist at Marlboro College, Vermont. For a discussion on class relations of aesthetic theory, see Gene H. Bell-Villada, "The Idea of Art for Art's Sake: Intellectual Origins, Social Conditions, and Poetic Doctrine," *Science and Society* 50, (winter 1986): 415–39.

4. M. H. Abrams, "Art as Such: Origins of the Modern Theory of Literature and the Arts" (address presented to the Miller Committee, University of Illinois, Champaign, 1981).

5. "Making the World Safe for Elitism: Multiculturalism in Art Equals Middlebrow Kitsch," *Washington Post,* June 27, 1993.

6. Jane Tompkins, *Sensational Designs,* discusses the creation and maintenance of artistic canons, especially from a cui bono perspective.

7. Beardsley, *Aesthetics,* pp. 140–63.

8. Michael Owen Jones, *The Hand-Made Object and Its Maker* (Berkeley: University of California Press, 1975), pp. 218–21.

9. For a significant description of what happens in the clash between those with aesthetic power and those without, see Casey Nelson Blake, "An Atmosphere of Effrontery: Richard Serra, *Tilted Arc,* and the Crisis of Public Art," in *The Power Culture: Critical Essays in American History,* ed. Richard Wightman Fox and T. J. Jackson Lears (Chicago: University of Chicago Press, 1993).

10. Lawrence Levine, *Highbrow/Lowbrow: The Emergence of Cultural Hierarchy in America* (Cambridge: Harvard University Press, 1988), p. 255.

11. Barbara Hernstein Smith, *On the Margins of Discourse* (Chicago: University of Chicago Press, 1978), esp. "The Ethics of Interpretation," pp. 133–56.

12. Kenneth Ames, *Beyond Necessity: Art in the Folk Tradition* (Winterthur, Del., 1977), p. 16.

13. George Kubler, *The Shape of Time: Remarks on the History of Things* (New Haven: Yale University Press, 1967).

14. "What is called playful by those favorably inclined and is condemned as child's play by the serious . . . actually has profound significance. By detaching things from their familiar context, by considering them from hitherto unknown points of view, by employing them without obvious purpose but out of sheer joy in totally different combinations, a resilient creative power is kept alive. And this is what mankind needs when the freezing point has been reached in a tradition which finds itself no longer capable of meeting a newly emergent problem" (Ulrich Conrads and Hans Sperlich, *Fantastic Architecture,* quoted in Starsmore, *English Fairs,* p. 95).

15. Discussions of festival theory and definitions are to be found in Barbara Babcock, ed., *The Reversible World: Symbolic Inversion in Art and Society* (Ithaca, N.Y.: Cornell University Press, 1978); Richard Bauman, ed., *Folklore, Cultural Performances, and Popular Entertainments: A Communications-Centered Handbook* (New York: Oxford University Press, 1992); Roberto Da Matta, "Carnival," in *Secular Ritual,* ed. Barbara Meyerhoff and Sally Falk Moore (Assen: Van Gorcom, 1977); Larry Danielson, "The Ethnic Festival and Cultural Revivalism in a Small Midwestern Town" (Ph.D. diss., Indiana University, 1972); Falassi, *Time Out of Time;* Henry Glassie, *All Silver and No Brass: An Irish Christmas Mumming* (Bloomington: Indiana University Press, 1976); John J. MacAloon, ed., *Rite, Drama, Festival, Spectacle: Rehearsals toward a Theory of Cultural Performance* (Philadelphia: Institute for the Study of Human Issues, 1984); Manning, *The Celebration of Society;* R. J. Smith, *The Art of the Festival* (Lawrence: University Press of Kansas, 1971); Richard Swiderski, *Voices: An Anthropologist's Dialogue with an Italian-American Festival* (Bowling Green, Ohio: Bowling Green State University Popular Press, 1987); Victor Turner, *The Ritual Process;* and *Western Folklore* 31, no. 4 (Special Festival Issue, 1972).

16. See Alan Dundes and Alessandro Falassi, *La Terra in Piazza* (Berkeley: University of California Press, 1975), esp. pp. 142–161.

17. See Ian T. King, "Political Economy and the 'Laws of Beauty': Aesthetics, Economics, and Materialism in Marx," *Science and Society* 55 (fall 1991): 323–35.

Index